W9-AXJ-034

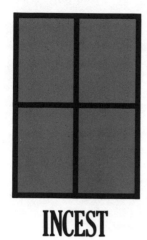

INCEST

ANNA KOSOF

INCEST

FAMILIES IN CRISIS

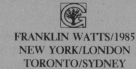

FRANKLIN WATTS/1985
NEW YORK/LONDON
TORONTO/SYDNEY

Library of Congress Cataloging in Publication Data

Kosof, Anna.
Incest: families in crisis.

Includes index.
Summary: Exposes the problem of incest in families and
discusses what can be done to prevent and treat this
problem. Also suggests further public involvement and
funding for the treatment of incest and other sexual
abuse of children.
1. Incest—United States.   2. Incest—United States—
Prevention.   3. Victims of incest—United States.
[1. Incest.   2. Child molesting]   I. Title.
HQ72.U53K67   1985   306.7'77   85-8920
ISBN 0-531-10071-5

Copyright © 1985 by Anna Kosof
All rights reserved
Printed in the United States of America
6   5   4   3

364.153
K-84

61014

Mitchell College Library
New London, Conn.
06320   Tel. 443-2811

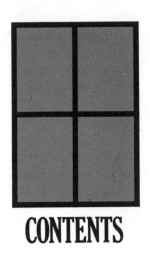

CONTENTS

I would like to thank all the people who gave so generously to the making of this book. Needless to say, it could not have been written without the personal stories of so many people.

However, some people must be singled out, because their contribution was invaluable. I must thank the members of the Virginia Beach Chapter of Parents United for their time and patience. They spent many painful moments with me, sharing their experiences in detail. I thank Fae Denton, who made much of that experience possible. Her insights were essential. I must also single out Dr. Rashmi Skadegaard for taking the time to share her knowledge and her many years of experience.

I could not forget the many victims who tried so hard to explain the experience of incest, an experience that no one can fully understand without having lived through the horror.

I thank them singly and collectively.

I also would like to thank Adrian Jones for helping me with the research for this book. Her work made a real difference.

Finally, I must thank Dr. Vincent J. Fontana for his advice and counsel throughout the writing of this book.

*Dedicated to the victims
and to Del
for listening so patiently*

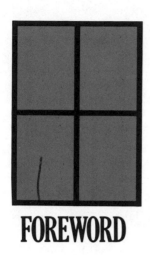

FOREWORD

by Vincent J. Fontana, M.D., F.A.A.P.
Medical Director, New York Foundling Hospital
Center for Parent and Child Development
Chairman of the Mayor's Task Force on Child
Abuse and Neglect, City of New York
Author of *Somewhere a Child Is Crying*

The statistics on the sexual abuse of children are staggering. In 1982, the American Humane Association in Denver reported 56,607 substantiated cases of sexual abuse of children. It is estimated that today one out of every three girls under 18 and one out of every eight boys under 18 have experienced some form of sexual abuse.

We do not know nearly enough about the sexual abuse of children and its causes and effects. One of the difficulties in gathering information on incest, for example, is that such incidents are frequently not reported. Nevertheless, we are beginning to learn more about it, largely because some of the victims in their desperation are turning to school counselors, friends, child protective agencies, and the police; and because society is at last willing to address the issue of incest.

We do know that incest cannot take place within a healthy family environment. We know, too, that incest is a relationship among at least three persons, the two active participants and the other parent. In some cases the victim fears that the other parent will not serve as a shield against the abuse, that it is not within that parent's power to protect the child, and that the adult can then easily intimidate and threaten the child into silence.

Children learn behavior patterns from their parents and their environment. Children who have been raised in an atmosphere of violence tend to become violent themselves. Children who are abused tend to abuse other children and to continue this pattern into adulthood, when they may also commit incest. As adults, in the role of parent, relative, or caretaker, these former victims have the opportunity to abuse children sexually. And the cycle of abuse continues.

As caring human beings we should be providing adequate protection for abused children. But sometimes the good intentions of a society are not enough. Innocent victims of incest and sexual exploitation are being further hurt by our failure to intervene. This failure is not due to a lack of knowledge but rather a lack of commitment to act on what is known. The problem is compounded by a lack of coordination, communication, and cooperation among the various agencies responsible for child protection in this country.

There is also a debate over the most effective or most appropriate means of intervention in cases of incest. The possibility that intervention and the method of offering help may fail or even hurt the victim is greater than we wish to acknowledge.

It is important, however, that those caught within the web of a troubled, incestuous family learn how to get the help they need. Treatment programs for victims, their families, and the offenders are essential. Without treatment, victims of child sexual abuse are at high risk of experiencing such teenage problems as delinquency, suicide, and unwanted pregnancy. Without help, these victims might, in turn, become abusers.

The publicity given to incest is fairly recent. Books, newspaper articles, TV shows, movies—all have dealt with this issue. Incest is perhaps the last type of child abuse to be recognized as a serious, widespread problem.

This book highlights and exposes an all-too-long hidden malady, and serves to increase our understanding of incest—what can be done to prevent it and to treat it. It is to be hoped that Ms. Kosof's message will further serve to increase resources for treatment of child sexual abuse. Individual involvement and funding for treatment are the most important responses in the battle against incest—a crime against children and a national shame.

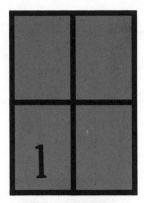

THE CRIME
OF INCEST

In 1976, I sat with a group of teenagers. One girl told the group that she ran away from home because she was a victim of incest. A fourteen-year-old girl who sat next to her looked puzzled. "What's that? 'Incext'? How do you spell it?"

In 1984, I sat with another group of teenagers. They knew the word. They thought that it only happened to people in other countries. Some believed that it was common among primitive societies, while others thought that only very crazy people could commit incest. For the most part, they were embarrassed. It seemed like a "dirty" subject. Some giggled, some were afraid to look up, as if we were talking about something unmentionable. Well, in a way we were. We were talking about the most universal of all taboos, "incest." (A *taboo* is something that is traditionally forbidden.)

Incest taboo exists in numerous variations, but all cultures prohibit intercourse and marriage within the "nuclear family," that is, between parent and child and between brothers and sisters.

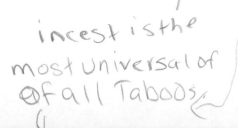

What is incest? In this book I am applying a broader definition of "incest." Our definition of incest reflects a psychological, rather than a biological, legal, or social concept of the taboo. Incest is defined as any sexual relationship between a child and an adult with parental responsibilities; or between two siblings. From a psychological point of view it does not really matter if the child and the adult are not related. What matters is the relationship that exists between the adult and the child or between brothers and sisters.

We further define a sexual relationship to mean any physical contact that has to be kept a secret. From a legal point of view, for a relationship to be considered incestuous there must be sexual intercourse. That narrow view is reflected in most state laws and in popular thinking. But incest can also mean fondling, touching, oral sex, or any other sexual activity. When a parent initiates the child into activities which serve a sexual interest, where a secret relationship is created, the bond between the parent and child is corrupted.

Most psychologists believe that while intercourse may be the worst form of incest, any sexual activity that has to be kept a secret, hidden from others, is damaging to a child. The same argument applies to brother-sister relationships. Any activity involving an overt sexual relationship is believed to confuse and distort the natural love between the siblings.

Most state laws recognize stepparents within the incest code. For example, Georgia law states: "Person who engages in sexual intercourse with a known relative, by blood or marriage; father, daughter or stepdaughter, mother, son or stepson; brother and sister of the whole or half blood; grandparent and grandchild; aunt and nephew, uncle or niece. Penalty: minimum one year, maximum twenty years."

While the laws vary from state to state, the extent of the penalty can vary from a fine to one year in jail or to a life sentence. One thing is the same—incest is against the law in every state.

While some incestuous relations continue for a period of several years, it is still incest even if it happens only once. It doesn't have to involve sexual intercourse or physical force to be considered incest.

Incest has been a subject of fascination for psychologists, novelists, anthropologists, sociologists, historians, and lawyers. Much has been written about it, but interestingly, very little is known about it. There have been many studies, but these were usually based on a limited number of cases. It is only recently that we have begun to see enough concrete studies to be able to make statements without contradictions.

For example, according to almost all studies, in incestuous relationships 97 percent of the offenders are men, and 90 percent of the victims are women. In other words, most incestuous relationships are between the father or stepfather and the daughter. At least, that is the commonly held view. But researchers agree that there are far more female offenders than the 3 percent reported. Some suggest that number is closer to 10 percent. However, in this book we are focusing largely on the male offender and the female victim, because that is clearly far more common than incestuous relations between mother and son. Some experts have such differing opinions about the profile of the mother that we can only offer some of those opinions. There really have not been enough statistics gathered to make definitive statements about their pattern.

Information about sibling incest is also very scarce, although it is known that more of it occurs than is reported—for several reasons. For instance, it is very difficult for most children to tell their parents that they have been involved in a secret relationship. If the brother used force and the female is an involuntary participant, she might be afraid to tell on her brother. She might feel she was putting the parents in a situation where they would have to choose between their children. If the female is a voluntary participant, she might feel very responsible. Boys are even more reluctant to disclose incestuous relations. They often try to block the situations out of their minds.

This book focuses on incest apart from child sexual abuse.

Incest is just one form of child abuse. Child sexual abuse does not necessarily involve sexual relations with a parent or a sibling. In this book, I have only included those relations that are incestuous, based on the definition given earlier.

In this examination of incest I also will not touch on sexual relations between cousins. There is no universal prohibition against sexual relations between cousins. In fact, among some groups, marriage between cousins is preferred. Even in the United States there is no consistent prohibition against relations with cousins.

What I will try to do is give a clear picture of the issue. There are many variations, many stories, some that have never been told.

For this book, I interviewed victims of incest. I also spoke with offenders and with mothers of victims. Their stories were different, but all spoke about the terrible "secret" they had kept. This book will explore the terrible secret of incest.

I talked to one victim after she finished reading the manuscript for one of the chapters. She commented, "It was not like that at all. You said that most victims don't want to put their parents in jail. I *did* want my father to go to prison. My father was not as 'nice' as you seem to make some of those guys appear."

She was right. For every story or situation in this book, there are many others that do not fit the pattern at all. Some of the offenders were violent, very abusive both physically and mentally, while some victims had a close relationship with their fathers. Some offenders are sexually disturbed or deranged. Some molest more than one child, while many others do not. Some offenders were in and out of mental institutions, while some misplaced their love with their children. Some of them started committing incest with two-year-old children, and others began when the children reached puberty. This book highlights the most common patterns.

While the laws are very strict, very few offenders serve

prison sentences. Some are in programs for sex offenders, while others are in therapy or on probation. Some are serving life sentences; others have gone unpunished.

Some families stayed together after the incest was exposed, while many families split apart. Some of the victims are struggling with serious psychological problems; some have been hospitalized; some have developed multiple personalities, whereby they function as two or more distinctly different persons. Yet, many appear to function perfectly well, and no one knows that they were once victims of incest.

One thing is certain: In the past few years incest has received increasingly more attention. Every day we learn more about this issue because children are coming forward more and more frequently. In the past, these relationships often continued for as long as eight or ten years. Now many victims are reporting the incidents. They are less afraid to tell, and they think that now there is a better chance that they will be believed. Clearly, there are major changes going on. Not so long ago, highly respected psychologists believed that incest was only in the minds of the children. Now, not only do we know that it exists, but we also know that very few children lie about this subject.

The experts with whom I talked all agreed on some issues. First, *the victim is never to blame*. It is exclusively the responsibility of the adults to govern their behavior, particularly when they are supposed to give guidance and be a parent to a child.

Second, the experts pointed out that *it is important that the victim tell somebody*. The story may not have a happy ending. When the secret is exposed it becomes a legal issue, to be handled by the authorities. That involves police, lawyers, judges, and sometimes even a court trial. But it is important that children feel that they can tell somebody. They should not enter adulthood bearing the psychological scars of incest.

Another message that must be conveyed is that *it has*

happened to many children. If you are a victim of incest, you are not alone. Incest is far more common than anyone has imagined.

Finally, there is not just one picture of the victim or the offender. *There are many variations of incest,* many stories to be told.

It is only when the secret is out that we can begin to understand incest. It is only when the victims can share their pain that we can learn more about the causes and the damaging effect that incest has on the victim. We do know that it is a very painful and difficult subject. The damage may linger for many years.

No, this book may not have a happy ending. Incest hurts. But there is help available. Victims can not only survive, they can overcome the anger and the hurt that this experience causes.

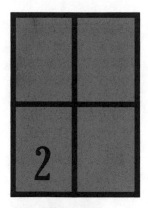

WHY THE
TABOO?

Anthropologist Margaret Mead defined incest as "the infraction of the taboo upon sexual relations between any two members of the nuclear family except husband and wife, that is between parents and children or any sibling pair." While no single definition of the taboo applies among all people, in some societies the definition may be broadened to include cousins and other extended family members. All cultures prohibit intercourse and marriage within what is known as the "nuclear family." Therefore, the incest taboo serves to distinguish between those with whom sexual relations are forbidden and those with whom they are permitted. It is called a "taboo," rather than a "prohibition," because its violation is viewed with a special sense of intense horror.

While some societies believe that a man can marry as many wives as he can afford, and others consider that the preferred marriage partner is the maternal cousin, the incest taboo is universal. It is one of the few things on which, throughout history, all societies seem to agree.

How and why did this taboo start? Like everything else about incest, there are many explanations. First, there is a biological explanation—the fundamental purpose of the incest taboo is to prevent inbreeding. This theory really regulates reproduction. It is believed that inbreeding is biologically harmful to offspring, causing mental retardation and other problems.

It is, however, the psychological and social explanation for incest that seems to make even more sense. According to sociologists and anthropologists, the taboo exists to establish the necessary conditions for family life—to regulate sexual conflicts and rivalries and therefore to create an appropriate environment for the socialization of children.

Just think, if, in one family, a father were to marry his daughter, or the mother her son, it would very quickly dissolve the family. We would never create new families, new ties with other social groups. The taboo is considered necessary to ensure the successful passage from childhood to maturity. It is also necessary that enough children grow to be adults and carry on their function as members of society. Each time a person marries a member of another family, a new kinship has been created. The joined groups are now able to cooperate with each other as a family.

According to the anthropologist Levi-Strauss, the incest taboo during the early development of society had less to do with the prohibition of marriage with mother, sister, or daughter than a rule obliging the mother, sister, or daughter to be given to others. Levi-Strauss maintained that it was the process of marrying out of one's family that enabled societies to survive and grow. Each family that married into another created a new network of cooperation. Since one would not wage war with one's own family, new dependencies assured peace.

Therefore, the incest taboo is argued on several levels. First, it is believed to be biologically harmful to humans to produce offspring from the same nuclear family. It is believed to be essential to the psychological socialization of the child to have the incest taboo. Finally, it is believed to be essential to society as we know it to create social networks.

"A society which allowed incest could not develop a stable family; it would therefore be deprived of the strongest foundations for kinship." This view is presented by B. K. Malinowski, one of the most famous social scientists.

Some anthropologists go even further. They say that widespread failure to observe the incest taboo is an index of the disruption of a society that may be even more significant than the more usual indicators—crime, suicide, and homicide rates. In other words, the health of a society can be judged on the degree to which its members adhere to the incest taboo. It has been suggested that a society that has a lot of crime and disorder is failing in some respect. In this case, some people believe that something as universal as the incest taboo is a better indicator. The breakdown of such a taboo is equated to a general breakdown in society.

Some statistics suggest that one in every ten people in this country is a victim of incest. Why is incest so prevalent? Clearly, no one has the answer to that question, but some suggestions have been presented. First, this society has an enormous amount of stress caused by poverty, unemployment, and alienation. There is also a large problem with alcohol and drug abuse. Sexual taboos, in general, have relaxed. Experts think these factors influence the growing rate of incest.

Other social scientists suggest that the breakdown of the family structure has contributed to the problem of incest. Traditionally, aunts, uncles, and cousins were a part of everybody's family. If you didn't turn to your mother, you could talk to your aunt, your grandmother, or someone else in the family. That structure is no longer in place. Families are more isolated. The growing rate of divorce has also helped to splinter families. Sometimes a family is headed by a single parent. New and transient relationships can contribute to abuse. With all these changes, many children are missing their foundation, the family structure.

Is there more child abuse in the United States than in other countries? No one knows the answer. There is abuse in Western countries, but how much of it goes on in other parts of the world is difficult to determine. We can only guess. Social scientists believe that it goes on everywhere, but they assume that a significant number of divorces, isolated nuclear families, and a lack of an extended family contribute to the rate of incest.

We all have a lot of questions but few answers about what causes incest. It will take a few more years before we know enough about the pattern of incest to be able to understand its causes.

Let's look now at some of the victims of incest. Let's listen to their stories.

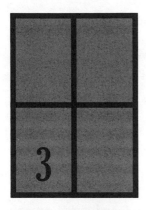

THE VICTIM

"Why didn't you tell your mother?" I asked Michelle.

"How could I tell my mother? How could I tell my mother that her husband, my father, had been having sex with me since I was eight years old?"

Michelle is now sixteen years old, painfully thin, with deep sunken brown eyes. Like most victims of incest, she had felt tormented and confused by an overwhelming desire to tell somebody, to end the nightmare. Yet she felt unable to tell her mother, so she lived with the secret.

"He told me that if I ever told anyone, he would kill me. At times, I wake up at night still wondering if he'll kill me. I think that till the day I die I'll be afraid of that man."

Incest began when Michelle was eight years old. As is usually the case, it began with touching, fondling, and "playing."

As a little child, Michelle was very close to her father. They went fishing together, to the store together; she sat on his lap. She remembers her father as warm and affectionate to her. She always felt that she had a special relationship with him.

"Did you enjoy your relationship with him?"

"At that time I did. When I was eight or nine, I enjoyed the attention, the love, and the special affection. He told me that it was just between us, that no one would ever know. He implied that all little girls have a special relationship with their fathers. That's why none of the other little girls ever talked about it.

"At that time, my brothers would get whipped, my mother was very uncommunicative and withdrawn, so my father was all I had. He would sometimes come home and if things were not to his liking, both my brothers got a beating. My mother would go to church. And that's when my father's attention would turn to me."

Like most incest victims, Michelle has hazy memories about what happened. The incidents usually occurred at night, often while Michelle was either asleep or pretending to be asleep.

"I never knew when he would come into my room. I think that sometimes it seems like it happened every night, then sometimes I think that it happened maybe once a month or twice a year. I really cannot remember."

Michelle came from a family with two brothers and a father who worked as a factory foreman. Her mother took care of the family and was a prominent member of the local church. On the surface, Michelle's family seemed very ordinary.

Her father paid all of the household bills and made most of the decisions concerning the family. No one argued with him. It was his household, his wife, his children. Michelle, like her mother, respected and obeyed that authority. Although at age nine Michelle enjoyed the special attention she received from her father, that same attention became very possessive as she grew older.

"I literally could not walk out of the house without my father wanting to know where I was going, with whom, and when I would be back. I could not date boys, and I desperately wanted to end the relationship I had with my father. I hated him by then."

Michelle was an A student in her early years in school but her grades started slipping. She started skipping school. She wouldn't eat regularly and constantly kept hurting herself by falling and banging her head. She broke her ankle and developed a nervous stomach.

"Didn't your mother think that there was something wrong?" I wondered.

"She did, but she didn't really know what. I figured that as long as I was sick my father would leave me alone. I also figured that my mother should have known what was going on. I really hated her too. I somehow felt that if she ever opened her eyes, she would have seen. She should have known. But my mother was the kind of woman who couldn't tell you that having periods is a normal part of a woman's life.

"I'll never forget—one day I came home from school early. I told my mother that I was throwing up. She gave me a lecture about eating pizza and spending too much time with my best friend, Lisa. At that time I almost told her, as she went back to making her daily grocery list, searching the house for a discount coupon."

Most female victims of incest feel very estranged from their mothers. It is a complicated relationship, full of guilt, anger, distance, loneliness, and a feeling of deep betrayal. Most girls believe that their mothers should have known what was going on and protected them. Though many victims readily admit that their mothers did not "know," they feel that somehow their mothers should have been perceptive enough to see that something was wrong. So they deeply resent their mothers for not being "mothers," the ones who protect their offspring.

The feeling of guilt is also very common. Living in the same house, being the "other woman," sleeping with the mother's husband produces the greatest feeling of shame, of guilt and helplessness. Victims of incest don't necessarily feel that they are victims. Many feel that in some way, they are to blame, that they are responsible. They feel powerless and angry with themselves for being too weak to confront the situation.

"Did you ever say no to your father?"

"I couldn't. That's the other feeling that tears you apart. I fantasized for days about talking to my father, telling him to stop. Asking him to stop. I never did. I could never say no to him. At least once a week I thought about committing suicide, but I still couldn't say no. Instead, I became more and more angry with myself and my mother."

Incest changes the normal process of development during adolescence. While most teenagers talk about exploring sexuality, giggling about kissing and hugging, incest victims feel totally isolated and alone.

"How are you going to sit with kids and talk about your first 'french kiss,' or that some boy tried to open your bra, when you have been having intercourse with your father. One day, I was talking to a couple of my girl friends about getting pregnant. I said something about how the vagina expands, so that intercourse could happen. My friends looked at me and laughed. 'Boy, how would you know anything, you haven't even really kissed a boy yet.' Well, I turned red. What are you supposed to say to that?"

Incest during the early teenage years seems to affect the victims in one of two ways. Either they are unable to form a relationship with a member of the opposite sex or they have numerous casual sexual encounters.

Unlike Michelle, Judy, now 19, often had sexual relations with older boys.

"It really didn't mean anything to me. If a guy wanted to sleep with me, I would let him. I felt absolutely worthless. It didn't matter if I slept with one or ten guys, since I wasn't a virgin anyway. It was the only way that I knew to get back at my father, who always had a fit if I went out with a guy. I would come home, get punished, and yelled at, and I continued to do it anyway. I think that it was the only form of affection I knew. Then I got pregnant. I had an abortion. When my father tried to have intercourse with me, I told him I couldn't because I had had an abortion. He called me all kinds of names, 'bitch,' 'slut,' 'whore,' 'no good son of a bitch.' That's when I told my mother."

But as in many other cases, Judy's mother did not believe her. She called Judy a liar and ordered her out of the house.

"I was sixteen when I went to live with a distant relative. Then I married a guy, who, like my father, terrorized and abused me. I got pregnant, had a child and, after two years of marriage, got divorced.

"I felt that I was the lowest person on earth. I was made to feel that no one would ever want me, that I was lucky that someone would even marry me. Even though my husband was verbally abusive and physically violent, and drank too much, I was grateful at first to be married."

"Is there a difference between the impact that incest has on a female victim and a male victim?" I asked various experts. While no one liked to make generalizations because the impact can vary tremendously, some tendencies have been noted.

Female victims tend to turn their problems inward. Some later become involved in prostitution, while many girls become addicted to drugs and alcohol. According to some unsubstantiated reports, a significant number of the women become nuns. As one nun, who is also a therapist, said to me, "It was my only way to deal with my sexuality."

Again, a significant number of female victims grow up to be either asexual or homosexual. A woman in her late twenties said that she had relations with other women because every time she became sexually involved with a man, the experience with her father came to mind. She was simply unable to separate the two experiences.

The boys, however, exhibit antisocial behavior that is more outwardly directed. They become violent, juvenile delinquents and abusers. There is concern that the child sexual abuser is getting younger and younger in age. It is believed that many of them become abusers because they were themselves abused as children.

Some victims of incest develop multiple personalities. They create several distinctly different personalities, whereby they can divorce themselves from reality and become someone else. It is almost as if they wish to divorce themselves from their bodies.

"I hated myself. That's why I developed two of me. I lived that way for years. After about three years with a psychiatrist, I began to put the two people (in me) together," explained one victim.

But there is no one answer that can be given about the impact of incest. Certainly, some factors make a major difference—how long the abuse continued, the age of the child, the relationship that he or she had with the adult, whether or not the relationship involved intercourse, and the aftermath once the incest was exposed. Not all victims become psychotic or develop multiple personalities. In fact, only a small number of victims have such extreme responses. Not all of the victims are exposed to intercourse. Also, some of the offenders have been able to say that they were the ones responsible, that they were deeply sorry, while some of the children have had to face court trials, and have been accused publicly of lying. It is believed that the older the child, the more serious the impact. It is argued that if the victim is young and if the incest does not involve intercourse, the child may not suffer as deeply as in cases where it is prolonged into the teenage years.

Some victims have grown up never being able to have a normal sexual life, while there are thousands who have never told anyone, but are seemingly living a normal life. Of course, we know nothing about these silent victims.

Incest occurs in all types of families. It seems to cut across economic, professional, and racial lines. It is true that some male offenders have a drinking problem, while others are violent and abusive. Some mothers work outside the home, others are housewives. It seems true that most of the fathers are the dominant figure in the family, but not all the mothers are passive and submissive.

Judy's family, for instance, fell into the more extreme category. Her father often came home drunk and violent. Everyone was afraid of him. Unlike Michelle, Judy never experienced any real affection from her father, and mostly hated him for what he did to her. She felt no special bond with her mother or anyone else in her immediate family. Her brother, several years older, also beat her regularly, particularly when he was hit by their father.

"My mother almost never stood up for us. When my father would beat us, she would just try to leave the room. Of course, she never stood up for herself, so how could I expect her to stand up for us. She made it a habit not to be home too much, so when she wasn't home, I had to do the cooking and make sure that my father got fed. I was like a surrogate wife."

Incest in Judy's life started, she thinks, when she was about six or seven years old. Her father would come in at night, fondle her, and leave. That continued, she believes, off and on until she was about eleven.

"Sometimes I don't know how much of it was a nightmare and how often it happened in reality. Usually, I was asleep or pretending to be asleep while he was doing it to me. When I was about eleven, my mother had to go visit her ill mother for a few weeks. I begged her to take me with her, but she said that I had to help with my brother and my father. Of course, they couldn't cook an egg. I stayed home. My father came home late one night. That night I was scared. I somehow knew that with my mother gone, he could do something. This time it wasn't just touching and feeling me inside. He had intercourse with me while I cried and screamed. He kept telling me to shut up or I would wake my brother. To this day I don't know how my brother can claim that he didn't know what was going on. He was in the next room. But I guess he was afraid of my father, too. That night he smelled like alcohol, he was like a crazed man.

"I told him that I would tell my mother if he did that again. He told me that no one would ever believe me, that they would send me away to a mental institution and lock me up. I believed him, so I didn't tell anyone. It went on until I was about fourteen, when he beat me."

As a teenager, Judy drank and smoked marijuana. She worked part-time, and stayed away from home as much as possible. Her father was often out of work and at home during the day. Her parents would have on-going fights, particularly when her father was out of work. When he got angry, he would slap his wife, but every time his wife threatened to divorce him, his conduct would temporarily improve and she would stay.

"Once he moved out for a while and I thought that it might be permanent. I was relieved. I hoped that maybe my mother and I could talk to each other. Well, that lasted about two weeks. My mother was upset all the time that he was gone. She blamed my brother and me for his leaving. We never got to talk about anything. After that I started hanging out with kids who hardly ever went to school, got high on pot, and drank beer. I no longer cared."

Judy's father never really admitted the incest. Her mother probably knew that it was true. At least that's what Judy believes.

After Judy left home and got married, she thought that she would find love and affection with her nineteen-year-old husband, who worked as a shipping clerk. She hoped to find love with her own child. She wanted to be a better parent than the ones she had.

The marriage was a disaster. Her husband, like her father, drank, abused her, and could not face up to the responsibility of marriage.

"Boy, it really is true. So many women marry their fathers. I went through the whole experience all over again. I didn't think I deserved better," was Judy's explanation.

In a matter of a few years, Judy's husband left and joined the Air Force. She went on welfare and placed their child in foster care. Judy's now finishing a high school equivalency program, while attending counseling sessions.

"My father and I never speak to each other and my mother came to visit the baby only once. My brother is out in California, so all the support and help that I have come from my cousins and friends. My mom is still married to my father, and to this day, we have never talked about what happened. I think that it will take years, many years, to work through the incest part. Now, at least I have met other women who have survived incest, so I don't think that I am the only one in the entire world whose father did this to his daughter."

Almost all incest victims mention the feeling of isolation, that this could never happen to anyone but them. They feel like freaks. But once the incest secret is "broken," many of them feel that a big weight has been lifted from them. Often they feel that whatever happens, it cannot be as bad as living with the secret.

"Whatever else you feel, you want to love your parents. It's amazing how strongly you want to excuse them, protect them, take the blame for what happened. I wanted to love my father," said Michelle.

Michelle could never tell her mother, though some nights she practiced what she would say, how she would say it. But she couldn't do it. Her physical health deteriorated; her school grades continued to fall. She became very withdrawn and slept a lot.

One day Michelle's school counselor called her into her office for a "chat." Michelle said that "it" just came out. "I just burst it out of my system." No sooner did it come out than she realized that she had revealed the "secret" that her father said never to tell anyone. The secret that she had kept so well for so many years just "broke" in the office of a woman she hardly knew. "Oh, don't tell my mother, please! You can't tell my mother," she pleaded with the counselor.

"Well, she told me that she would have to tell my mother, that she would help me tell my mother, but all I could do was run to the bathroom and throw up."

The social worker called her mother; they both told her. Her mother was shocked and found it hard to believe Michelle. Essentially, she knew that it was true. Michelle wanted to run away. She said that this was the worst day of her life. For years, she wanted to tell somebody, but now that she did, she just wanted to die, to run away, never to see either of her parents again.

Michelle was sent to live with relatives, who were not aware of what had happened. "I just wanted to run away. Here I am again with some relatives who don't know. Again, I can't talk to anyone. I can't go home. I am afraid that my father will kill me, my mother will hate me. I just wanted to die."

Michelle's father did not admit the truth at first, but he turned himself in to the police and, after being questioned, confessed. The original indictment of statutory rape was reduced to a lesser charge. He was freed on probation, with therapy as one of the conditions of his probation.

"When I came back home, things were no better than when I left. Maybe even worse. My father moved out for six months. I was not allowed any contact with him. I knew that he was really angry with me. Living with my mother and my two brothers was very uncomfortable. My brothers were angry with me because their father was taken away for something that they seemed to think must have been my fault.

"My mother was simply unable to communicate. She was upset and crying a lot of the time. Then I think that she started to resent me for what happened. She really didn't know what to do, to stay with my father or divorce him. She still loved him, I think. I was the one who felt totally out of place, like I had a disease."

Michelle left home and moved in with her aunt, uncle, and cousins who lived in a nearby state. Her parents have since joined Parents United, a support group for parents who have lived through the horror of incest and can share their own experiences in a caring atmosphere.

Michelle has adjusted relatively well to her new environment. She misses her family, but she is not sure that she could live with her parents again. She is also in therapy. Aside from her immediate family, no one knows why she moved.

"I am torn again. I can't tell anyone here. I want to be normal. I want to be like everyone else. I don't want to be branded or teased. I don't want people to talk and whisper about me. So, I have not told anyone in school."

Michelle does see her mother periodically, though she has not seen her father in a year. She says that she can talk to her mother a little more easily now, but they still cannot talk about the incest.

"In a way, once the secret is out, what can you say about the incest part? Sometimes I think that my mother is waiting for me to say something, but I really don't know what to say. I am still uncomfortable talking about that part."

There is no way to really know how many victims of incest there are unless the "secret" is revealed. How many thousands of people are victims of incest who are still holding on to the "secret," who cannot tell anyone, who have grown up and are just coming to grips with it now, we will never know. According to one report, 58 percent of a group of women who were victims of incest left home without ever telling anyone.

What can we say about incest victims? What can we generalize about them? We can definitely say that incest is a very harmful experience. For one thing, not one female victim told me that she was not affected by incest or that she was affected in a positive way by the experience. The women with whom I talked felt an enormous sense of betrayal, a betrayal of love and trust. They wondered if they could trust anyone again after what they had been through.

In regard to this universal taboo I asked experts about the sister-brother relationship. "Is incest between a sister and brother as harmful as between parent and child?" "No" was the general opinion, but the answer is not that clear cut. Some argue that incestuous relationships between siblings can be as destructive as parent-child incest, depending on the circumstances and the age of the children. A key element is the duration and the level of force used in the relationship. But again we are reminded that incest of *all* types is damaging, even if it is between siblings.

I was surprised when I met people who had been involved in that type of relationship. I did not expect that the level of harm could be so deep. Angela, now forty years of age, just returned from a psychiatric ward.

"I committed myself into a hospital. I was totally unable to function."

Angela was one of those people who never dealt with her incestuous relationship with her older brother until she was in her late thirties. She was married for fifteen years, and her marriage ended.

"That's when my early childhood came back. I really never remembered anything. Even now, my memories are very hazy. I have been asking my older sister to fill in some blanks."

Incestuous brother-sister relationships seem to be in two different categories. Early experimentation between two siblings who are relatively close in age is considered very common and without any serious consequences. This type of behavior may involve some touching and fondling, but it does not involve sexual intercourse. Usually, children don't even remember some of these experiences as in the natural process of growing up, they soon turn their attention and their curiosity to peers outside of the family.

The second type of behavior is the one that seems to cause damage. This type of relationship involves many complicated emotions and a more overt sexuality between the siblings. Often, it involves some degree of physical or psychological force.

"Angela, why did you continue a relationship with your brother?"

This relationship, like many others involving siblings, pointed to the children's inability to have a close relationship with either parent. They were unable to relate to other children and unable to communicate with their parents. They developed an emotional attachment for each other that continued until their teenage years. Again, Angela's memory was very hazy and she could only give a very sketchy picture.

"We developed a world of fantasy, a world full of guilt and confusion. When we became teenagers, the relationship took a new turn. We both wanted to let go of each other, but we were afraid to let go. We were very dependent on each other.

"I guess, about the time I was thirteen or fourteen years old, it stopped. My brother became interested in sports with other boys and eventually, acquired a girlfriend. I was sort of left alone. We never talked about it. We never told anyone."

"It didn't have any effect on your brother?" I wondered. According to Angela, her brother has no memory of any of this experience. He is married and seems to have no problem with his incestuous background.

Angela had difficulty during her marriage because she remembered some of her relationship with her brother and seemed to find it difficult to get past the physical act.

"My brother would always tease me, laugh at me. I began to hate myself for being unable to say no. I am not even sure why I went along with it. But clearly, my brother and I were very close. Then he cut me out of his life. Then I had no one. I never see him now. I tried to talk about it to him and that just made it worse. Since he says that it is not true, I felt that I needed to come to grips with my past life. So, after six months of hospitalization, I feel great and I feel that I have come to understand the parts of my past that were a puzzle to me."

I wondered why the experience for Angela was so damaging. It did not involve intercourse, so that the fear of pregnancy was absent. While the damage was not in the same proportion as a parent-child relationship, the damage had to do with her own emotional relationship with her brother. They were unable to be close to their parents, they could not relate to outsiders. That they had to create a fantasy world is the part that caused so much of the confusion in Angela.

We know very little about sibling relationships until such

children reach adulthood. They usually don't talk to anyone about it. The relationship with their parents is usually very distant, creating in part the dependency on each other. They keep the secret to themselves. When one sibling then starts to break away, the other feels totally alone.

It seems that it is the emotional dependency rather than the physical elements of an incestuous sibling relationship that leaves the scars. Like the incestuous relationship between parent and child, a brother-sister relationship confuses lines of communication. It confuses roles and creates a "secret." Further, it interferes with the normal process of growing up, of exploring relationships with outsiders, of developing a natural love and trust with other children.

"I think that it's the other way around," a therapist pointed out. "The children are involved in an incestuous relationship because they cannot reach out, they cannot communicate with the parents, they are afraid of exploring the outside world. When these people grow up, they also cannot function on a day-to-day basis with the outside world. Every day that you go to work, you have to interact with the world. It is this process that they cannot handle. That's the real damage of sibling incest."

Some cases involve a great deal more pain than the case that we described. For Marjory, incest was physically abusive. Her brother was much older and used force and violence to obtain sex. She participated less voluntarily, but was unable to tell her parents. Like Angela, she only came to grips with it as an adult. Now in therapy, she has tried to examine the damage that the relationship has caused.

"For one, I cannot talk to my brother about it. I told my mother, who seems to feel that if I didn't tell her back then, I should try to forget about it now."

The greatest problem that Marjory feels is her inability to say no. Her fear of authority, fear of large men, and the feeling that something is wrong with her has stayed with her. She is just now learning to examine how she feels about things and do what she wants, not what others want her to do.

While most experts agree that the most damaging form of incest is between a parent and a child, the reason that the other forms of incest can cause harm is due to the disorder and the distorted relationships that it can create.

Incest, in all forms, however, brings together some of the most complex relationships in one "act." Incest involves a man (in most cases) who is a lover, a "boy friend," a person who has shared physical intimacy, an act of occasional tenderness or immense physical pain, and a shared secret. If an adolescent of twelve or thirteen experienced a love affair with a stranger, that in itself would be difficult enough to handle at such an early age.

Incest by definition is committed with a parent or a person who has parental authority, or between members of the same family. Therefore, it violates the normal parental relationship between the child and both parents. If a child is committing incest with her father, not only does she no longer have a parent-child relationship with that parent, but she cannot have a normal relationship with her mother, who is, after all, the wife of the man with whom she is having a sexual relationship. In this sense her mother is a rival, the "other woman" in a love triangle, a situation that would be difficult enough for a grown person to handle. Here, a child is thrown into a role of a grownup without the support of either of the people who are supposed to be closest to her—her parents.

An incest victim is keeping a "secret," one that most children are not called upon to keep. It is a secret that she knows could possibly put her father in prison, break up the family, hurt her mother, and change their lives forever. So she carries a burden that even most grownups could not handle without support. "She is like a grown woman with the body of a child," said one mother.

She is unable to take part in the normal process of being a teenager, exploring and learning about sex and sexual warmth from peers. Most teenagers talk about sex and sexual relationships; it is a part of growing up, of learning about the opposite sex. That process cannot occur for an incest victim. Many either cannot form any dating relationships during their teens or they become promiscuous with boys, believing that sex is all any boy wants anyway.

Case studies indicate that almost all victims of incest believed that they were betrayed by their mother. They felt that if a mother always knows when you take a cookie from the cookie jar, how could their mothers not have known that for years their husbands visited their daughters in the deep of night.

Some victims were bitter because they felt that if given the choice, their mother would choose their father over them. At the same time many stated that they did not want to break up their parents' marriage. In fact, as they got older, they just wanted to leave home. Yet incest is hard to leave behind, because there are reminders of it in adult life, again and again. Many women marry men who remind them of their father, and once married, the memories return. Some cannot have a healthy relationship with their husband or any man at all.

Often, the issue of incest is not confronted, and the anguish lingers on. "All I wanted from my father was for him to say that he was sorry. I wanted him to ask himself how he could have done that to me, to a little kid. I think that then, I could have some peace."

This woman is now in her thirties, some fifteen years after the incest ended. Yet that apology has not been made. Her mother has since divorced her father (not because of the incest) and wants her daughter just to forget about it. "My mother cannot understand why I can't just go on with life."

But so many victims really can't forget until they have heard the apology.

"I can't forget about it. It will take years of therapy to work out the hate, the guilt, the blame, the anguish, the fear of the dark, of night, but most of all, my feelings toward men."

Many victims of incest still love their fathers very much. Often they search for what they feel they never had, a real father.

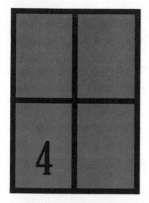

THE WORST DAY
OF MY LIFE:
THE MOTHER'S VIEW

"How could you really not know, Fran?" I asked in astonishment.

"I knew that something was wrong between Dick and me, but incest never entered my mind."

Dick interjected, "Fran really did not know. I was very careful; I didn't want to hurt Fran."

I wondered how he could say that. He insisted that he didn't want to hurt his wife, yet he carried on an incestuous relationship with his daughter for at least five years.

While most mothers in case studies of incest claimed that they did not know, in most incestuous relationships, the mother plays some part in the relationship. Usually, there is something missing in the husband-wife or mother-daughter relationship that makes the child feel that she cannot turn to her mother.

Dick and Fran have three children: two daughters and a son. As is frequently the case, incest occurred with the oldest daughter. This happened many years ago. She is now over twenty-one years old, married, and expecting a child.

"How could you have stayed married to Dick?" I asked a question that puzzles me to this day.

"I loved him" was the only answer offered. It was the answer that I heard repeatedly from women who stayed married to their husbands.

"I married him, I still love him. I know that my husband is really sorry about what he's done. We have both worked on this problem and on saving this relationship. He has really, really tried."

Fran seemed like a very caring mother. Even more confusing, her husband was a handsome, masculine Marine. Both of them were deeply religious (the Bible was prominently displayed on the coffee table). They lived in a very pleasant neighborhood. They looked like people who represented the best of American middle-class life. They were gracious hosts. They were willing to give me their weekend, to share their lives and their pain if it would help somebody.

The most common image of the mother in cases of incest is one of submission. According to most of the studies, she is passive and is dominated by her husband. She is also the role model for her daughter. Again, according to several studies, the men dominate and control the household. I think that while Fran and other women seemed to fit into this category, over all, some of the women were not so powerless or passive. They were certainly not without options.

"I'll never go back to what I was," Fran said with tears rolling down her face. "I can't go back to that."

"What were you like?" I wondered.

"Oh, I was a doormat. I did whatever Dick said. He controlled all of us. I could never go back to that."

Fran reaffirmed the stereotype of the passive wife of a domineering man, a man who gave orders at work and at home. This issue of the passive mother and the dominating father kept coming up in my interviews. I was puzzled. I asked several experts what the relationship was between passive/domineering parents and incest. They insisted that an unequally structured family unit promotes incest because the mother does not perform the role of an adult woman. She does not fully share in the decision making. There is a lack of communication that extends to the entire family. At the same time, she is a role model for her daughter.

("How can a girl feel that she can say no to her father when she has not heard her mother say no to him? How can she stand up to him as a child, when she has not seen her mother, a grown woman, stand up to him?) Fran asked.

(Several studies suggest that the mother in an incestuous family is unable to fulfill her traditional role. In one study, over half of the victims remembered that their mothers had periods of disabling illnesses that resulted in frequent hospitalization. Depression, alcoholism, and insanity were among the most common causes of the mothers' disabilities. Many of the victims described their mothers as uncommunicative or very detached. Some experts believe that a large percent of the mothers were themselves victims of sexual abuse or incest.)

Another general character of the incestuous family seems to be its large size. Repeatedly, we see that the number of children in these families is consistently higher than the national average. In one study, the number of children in the group was 3.6, well above the national average of 2.2 at that time. Another study of imprisoned incestuous fathers showed an average of 5.1 children.

Perhaps the size of the family and the general health of the mother may give us some insight into her passive and submissive nature. Encumbered with the care of many small children, often economically dependent, she is not in the best position to challenge her husband's authority. Some women saw no option but to stay. However, while some women may have believed that they had no option but to remain married, a significant number of women stayed with their husbands because they still loved them and felt that they could salvage their marriage. One mother said that she's been a failure all her life; therefore, she could not let her marriage fail as well.

Once the incest secret is revealed, the mother is often in

need of support and help. She is still the "mother," the "wife," the deserted "lover," and the one who is expected to keep the family together. She has to deal with the needs of the other children. But first, she has to decide whether to believe her daughter.

Some people wonder why a mother doesn't want to believe her daughter when the secret is broken. It's really simple. The mother has everything to lose by believing the daughter, but nothing to gain. If she believes her, she can lose her family, her husband, and the economic support. Then, the mother experiences feelings of hate and anger toward both her husband and daughter. A sense of confusion and disorientation takes over.

At first, a woman in this situation wants to divorce her husband. She feels betrayed. All of a sudden, the whole family is in crisis. Thoughts of welfare, financial support, social workers, and lawyers fill the hours. The mother feels that she must choose between her two roles—wife or mother. Should she support her daughter who is accusing her husband of a felony that could be punishable with a prison sentence or should she choose to believe that the child is lying?

Joan's story was typical. "We lived in this little town, next to the same people for eight years. They baby-sat for every one of my children. We drank hundreds of cups of coffee together. My husband went on fishing trips with Leah's husband. I was part of her extended family. She drove me to the hospital when I was pregnant. When the "secret" came out, they almost wouldn't speak to me. They couldn't even look at us. We were social outcasts. It really hurt. She is the person that I would have naturally turned to for some help and comfort. It wasn't there. It was as if they had become total strangers," Joan reminisced. "It was the worst day of my life."

Joan suddenly had the realization that there was something terribly wrong with her marriage. She tried to recall where things may have gone wrong, where she went wrong. Like so many mothers, she first blamed herself. She felt that she must have been a poor wife and not a very good mother. In a way, she wanted to know everything. How long did it go on; what happened; when did he first have intercourse with her daughter? Why didn't her daughter tell her? Why couldn't her daughter turn to her? Why didn't her husband turn to her for affection?

Then, like a switch, her mind turned it all off. She didn't want to know anything. In fact, she said, she fantasized about running away, never wanting to see her daughter or husband again.

"I realized that here I am confronted with incest, yet my daughter and I never talked about men or where babies come from. It was just like a nightmare. No one prepares you for the first night after the incest secret breaks. People talk about how to cry at funerals, but no one prepares us for this. We know where to turn if a loved one dies, but where do you turn when you have been totally devastated by your family?"

By this point, she was holding back tears, looking far away from her husband who was sitting uncomfortably on the sofa.

Like other mothers of incest victims, Joan came to realize that communication was never a major part of her life—not with her husband and never with her children. In fact, she really didn't know her daughter was acting "strange"; she could never sit and talk with her. Of course, it is common during the teenage years for there to be open hostility between mother and daughter, and acting "strange" is just "normal" at that time. "What teenager is not difficult, moody, and uncommunicative," said one mother. "But who would suspect incest?"

In the various studies done of incest victims, it is amazing how many of the victims described their mothers in less than flattering terms. Surprisingly, several of them talked about their fathers with much more affection and warmth.

"I didn't want to hurt my mother; that is why I never told her. But I also didn't think that she would support me or believe me. She was not a place for me to go. She was like ice to me," said one incest victim, an adult now who never exposed the secret.

Once the secret is out, there are numerous problems that the mother must confront. In most cases the husband was the breadwinner. How then will she handle the financial responsibilities by herself? If her husband is court-mandated to leave for a certain period of time, there is a serious question in her mind: "Can I make it on my own?" Then, the next issue that needs to be resolved is what to do with the daughter.

If the father stays home, the victim either cannot go home or is afraid to go home. Often, she is even uncomfortable with her mother, particularly when the mother-daughter relationship is one of hostility. She is afraid of what her mother may do to her. "Will she blame me? Will she think that I seduced him? What will my father tell her?"

While many daughters found their mothers uncommunicative and lacking in support, many of the mothers seemed really unhappy in their own lives. Some of them were oblivious to their children's needs and desires. It seemed like a vicious circle. The mother, because of her own status in the family, was in the midst of depression. Unable to provide the parental role of support, she made it very difficult for her child to turn to her at the time when she needed help. The relationship between the mother and daughter became more and more estranged and the distance between the two became difficult to bridge.

After reading so much about the submissive mother, as well as talking to victims about their perception of their mother, I wondered if all mothers were really so submissive and all fathers so domineering. Was that always the situation?

I asked this question of a therapist who had worked with hundreds of incestuous families. She replied with the expected no. But she added that all the families were impaired as a unit. Certainly, the root of some of the problems lies in the marriage. "Incest cannot breed in a healthy, good marriage where there is intimacy, closeness, and a give-and-take between all parties."

Other experts point out that it is wrong to blame the marriage, that by so doing the blame is placed on the wife, instead of the offender. They feel strongly that these men have sexual problems and that the therapy needed goes beyond what marriage counselors or group therapists can provide. They feel that these men are disturbed, and that the wives are not responsible for what happened.

Since so many victims of incest portray their mothers in a less than positive light, I began to wonder if any of them had had a strong mother-daughter relationship. Many of the mothers seemed blinded by their own situation, stuck with their own problems, so that they could not see what was going on around them. Perhaps some of them didn't want to see because they could not cope with their own lives. Some didn't know how to break the cycle.

Certainly, once the secret was out, many of the wives blamed themselves for what happened. They did feel immensely guilty and wanted to offer support to the daughter. They felt limited, overwhelmed by their own situation, their own marriage, and paralyzed by fear.

Both Fran and Joan had domineering fathers. Both married very domineering men. But many of the mothers I met with did not seem to be so submissive or the men so powerful. However, one therapist pointed out that most of the mothers had been a part of a self-help group for some time. They had been in therapy as well.

While Joan and Fran stayed married and tried to work out their relationships, Sue did not. She found out about the incest when she stumbled on the relationship. One night she came home too early. The evidence was blatant. She felt her world crumbling. She did not report the crime, though as we mentioned before, all states require that it be reported to the proper authorities.

She packed her children off to her mother, then she joined them herself. She left her husband and the children never saw him again. They later heard that he had died.

"I just wish that I had a chance to confront him. He died

without my ever telling him what he did to me," reflected one woman who was molested as a child.

The woman and her mother don't talk much about the incident. Her mother feels that she should try to get over it and forget about it.

This mother never wanted to save the marriage. She added, "I never wanted to see that creep again in my life. In fact, I wanted to kill him. I never wanted him near my children. What was there to save?"

It would not be accurate to ignore those women who did not try to save their marriages and believed that after incest there was nothing to save. Some therapists argue strongly that instead of trying to restore the family, it is more important for the mother to try to be supportive of the child and strengthen their mother-daughter relationship.

Several women, like Sue, never reported the incident, left their husband, and took the children away. However, we know very little about them. The reason that it is hard to know about them is that we only know about incest that has been reported, and that is believed to be less than 50 percent of the cases.

That's one of the reasons why it is difficult to make certain statements about incest. We only know a small part of the picture. We only know about those cases that have come to the public's attention.

Whether the victim's parents stay together or separate, it is crucial that the child feels that her mother is there for her support. So, again, it is the mother-daughter relationship that needs focus. Together they can survive this experience. They can survive incest.

THE MALE OFFENDER
THE FEMALE OFFENDER

I dreaded meeting the men. I could not imagine liking any one less than a man who hurt a child in such a painful and selfish way.

Incest is not committed exclusively by men, but according to almost all studies, men are the offenders in 97 percent of the cases, and females are the victims in about 90 percent of the cases. Again, this covers reported cases only. Most experts agree that women commit incest in larger numbers than those reported.

Wherever I went to talk to experts about incest, I asked about women who were the offenders and boys the victims. In each case, after a pause the response was a sigh, then "Oh, yes, there was a case last year, but I really don't know much about it." I came across some cases in the psychiatric records of women who seduced their sons. The women were described as deeply disturbed, and living in mental institutions. One woman is in prison, serving a sentence in Virginia. Allegedly, she was never convinced that she did anything really wrong. She claimed that her son was afraid of women and she felt that having sex with him would help him overcome his fears. She didn't want him to grow up liking men. The women in this category are usually alone with their children, without a man living in the house.

Then there are cases where some women abused their children with a male partner. But, known cases of women who commit incest are still rare enough to be singled out and remembered. Ironically, according to reported cases, there are more men committing incest with male children, than women who commit the same act with boys. In other words, men who have incestuous relations with their sons outnumber the women.

"Why is it that we have so few cases of incest committed by women?" I asked Flora Colao, an author and child abuse therapist. She disagreed with the statement, claiming that a lot more incest is committed than we know. She pointed to our different gender roles. If a man bathes his eight-year-old daughter every day, we would say that there is something wrong with what he is doing. When a woman does that with her son, we would not react in the same way. We might call her "overly protective," but we would probably not suspect anything beyond that. Clearly, physical contact with a mother is considered far more acceptable than with a father. In some cultures, mothers often fondle a male child's genitals to help him go to sleep. Usually this practice continues until the baby is one or two years old. Some children may not find in the behavior of a mother something that would suggest an incestuous relationship. However, incest very often can start at an early age with fondling and excessive touching and kissing that escalates to a more explicit sexual act.

The profile of the female offender is not as clear as that of the male, and very little has been written about her. As we mentioned before, she is usually alone with her children, and the boy seems to replace the man in her life. She seems to love the child deeply and has transferred the affection she might ordinarily feel for a man to her son. It is less threatening. Apparently, many of these women have been abused and hurt by men. They are afraid of men and turn to their own child because they feel loved and secure in that relationship. Some women abuse and hit the children and also have sexual relations with them. The children are usually in a state of total confusion, never knowing what act to expect. Some of the sexual acts can involve playing with the mother's breasts and fondling. Rarer cases involve sexual intercourse. Of course, intercourse with a young male child is almost impossible to achieve.

"What effect does incest have on a male child?" I asked Flora Colao. She confirmed the general picture presented by other experts, of a boy who is very confused about his own sexuality. If a male child was abused by his mother and if he did not enjoy the sexual activity, he is afraid that maybe it's because he doesn't like women. If he is abused by a male in the family, he might be frightened of being perceived as "gay." He wonders if perhaps he is signaling a preference for men. Why him? Why not another boy?

There is also another theory about the lower statistics involving female offenders that is again based on sex roles. Some experts believe that a boy is even more reluctant to expose his problems to a stranger than a girl is. Because there is usually no grown male figure in the household, the boy is often very attached to his mother. The mother is often his only parent. However, there are several male rapists serving time in prison with a past involving an incestuous relationship with their mother, something that was not revealed until after they were convicted and after many years in therapy. Clearly, the incestuous relationship had a very dangerous impact on them as children, yet they kept the secret for years.

I talked with the mother of a boy, now eighteen years old, who was a victim of incest with his father. She portrayed her husband as a man with a long history of serious psychological disorders, who drank heavily and was prone to violent behavior. Early in their married life, he had suffered a leg injury that left him slightly disabled. The family existed on his disability insurance.

When the mother found out about the incestuous relationship, she reported her husband to the police. He was tried, convicted, and sentenced to seven years in prison.

"Why didn't your son turn to you?"

She said it was because he was frightened of his father.

I wondered if that was the total answer. "Is your son homosexual?"

She flatly rejected the notion. He had a girlfriend with whom he lived and there seemed to be no indication that he was interested in men.

This woman was herself a victim of incest, as in many other cases involving the mother of the victim. She had a long history of being institutionalized. However, her story was confirmed by authorities. Apparently her son is adjusting well. He is not in therapy and has rejected counseling. Some counselors fear that the damage may be more apparent later.

"Many abusers have themselves been abused. We just hope that he does not become an abuser later in life. We are worried about the lack of help. He needs to talk to somebody about this," observed a therapist who is familiar with this case.

Domestic violence is another condition that could lead to incest. Some experts suggest that when a woman is physically abused by her husband, once the man is removed from the house, or the woman leaves, she might turn to her son for affection. Because the mother is in need of love but is afraid of men, the child becomes an easy target of incest. So far, there is no documented evidence that this pattern is common, but experts who are aware of some general signals are concerned about the damage that domestic violence can cause beyond the trauma of the violence itself.

Going back to the 97 percent of the offenders, the men— who are these people? When I first started my research, I didn't know what to expect. I didn't know what these men would look like. What could prompt a man to do that to a child, I kept wondering. Once, perhaps drunk, in the middle of the night, he might cause this to happen. But that is clearly not the pattern of incest. The abuse doesn't happen once, or only when the man is drunk or unable to remember his actions. It usually starts when the victim is eight or nine years old, and continues for several years. Intercourse is usually introduced when the child is around twelve. Of course, in some cases it starts earlier and continues for as long as ten years. So, we are not talking about incest as an act that happens once, a terrible crime never to be continued. It happens over and over, leading closer and closer to the ultimate sexual intimacy.

For years, these men committed adultery and incest at the same time, hurting both wife and child. They abdicated their parental role, yet at the same time knowing that if the secret ever got out, they could go to jail, they gave a unique power to the child. Incest is a crime in every state, punishable by years of imprisonment. In actuality it is rare that anyone serves years in prison for incest. Ironically, if a stranger raped a ten-year-old child, he could very likely serve fifteen years behind bars, while intercourse with a member of one's own family is treated less severely.

Those who wish to relieve the adults of blame like to suggest that teenage girls can be very seductive. There have been several famous books written about young girls seducing grown men who just cannot resist the sexual advances. Clearly, that argument is faulty on numerous grounds. Incest seems to start years before the child has reached puberty, at a time when a child is not sexually aware. Of course, the whole idea of blaming the victim is ridiculous. We as adults are supposed to take the responsibility for teaching and protecting our children. We are expected to be their trusted guardians. We are their role models.

The victims usually describe the men as very powerful, very strong and domineering. Of course, to a child, grown men do seem very powerful. Their sheer size can be intimidating. And while the children are clearly afraid of them, they keep the "secret" as a way of also protecting them. Remember, the victims are not only talking about their father, but a lover, often the only male figure that they have ever known.

So, from the victims we get a confused picture of a man they feel has hurt them, yet loved them.

Interestingly, men who commit incest usually tend not to fall into the category of pedophiles. Pedophiles are people who cannot engage in sexual relations with anyone but children. Most men who commit incest are generally not sex offenders against strangers, or rapists who use violent force. Yet they are involved with children, and they have committed rape, even though it is rare that force is used.

"My father raped me as far as I'm concerned," said Janice, now twenty-eight years old. "The fact that he was my father meant that he had absolute authority over me. I was taught never to say no to him. How could I have disobeyed a grown man? His sheer size was frightening to me. He was like a giant to me. He didn't need to threaten me with a gun at my head. Instead, he said that if I ever told anyone, he would go to jail, my mother could commit suicide, and I would be placed in a home for juvenile delinquents. Isn't that enough of a threat?"

What kind of person could do that to a child? We know that it goes beyond economic classes. There is incest among the middle, the lower, and the upper class. It cuts across racial and ethnic lines. It seems to occur all over the country, including small towns among people who would never come to a big city for fear of crime. It happens among people who are deeply religious, who speak about adultery with disgust. People commit incest who are grandfathers, who have wives and girlfriends. Some of the men are physically attractive and look powerful, while others seem unmasculine and less attractive. The majority of them are white but there are reports of incest in black families, too. Some of the men have serious sexual problems, some were physically abusive, and some were gentle.

I met only the men who are either in jail for their offense, or in some court-mandated therapy program for incest. The men that I met confessed to their crime with reluctance.

They have had to admit that they violated the world's universal taboo.

Steve, a small man, slightly built, seemed gentle and very pleasant in appearance. He looked like anybody you might meet on the street. He certainly did not appear violent or frightening in his demeanor. His daughter is now grown; he and his wife are divorced. The incest ended nearly six years ago, but he is still an active member of a program for incestuous families. He is a laborer, he has never been in trouble with the law, and had he not committed incest with his daughter, he would probably be very ordinary. Steve is an example of what many experts report. Child abusers were often victims themselves, and they tend to continue the cycle.

Steve claims that as a teenager he had been molested by a man and had a homosexual encounter that was abusive and exploitative. If there is any connection between that childhood incident and incest, we'll never really know. Many of the men stated that when they were children their homelife had been very violent, and beatings were part of a normal day. Steve tended to fall into the category of men who seemed gentle and weak.

Why did Steve turn to his daughter? He could only speculate. The men themselves cannot tell you what happened. Steve, like the other men, felt inadequate with other adults. He did not feel that he could hold his own with grown women. He felt that he was a poor husband.

At the same time Steve had a close relationship with his daughter. He loved her. He loved to take care of her. He liked to be in close physical contact with her. As his relationship with his wife deteriorated, his relationship with his daughter became closer and closer. He says that his daughter never complained or refused him sexually. His daughter was totally submissive, and therefore he believed that she was a willing participant. At times she enjoyed the special attention she received from her father. He clearly favored her over his wife or son. "She was my special little girl, my possession."

"You never thought that what you were doing was wrong, that you were hurting your daughter?" I wondered.

Like several other men with whom I talked, Steve rationalized his actions at that time with thoughts like: "I'm just initiating her into being a woman," or "She's also enjoying it. She never complained about what I have done."

The men who are not having intercourse with their daughter tend to rationalize the act with comments like, "But I didn't penetrate her. I didn't harm her. I was just touching. That doesn't do any harm."

"It's also like an obsession. You look forward to it, you are also making arrangements. It's like children playing games. We shared a secret. Incest also produces a real departure from reality. You begin to live the fantasy. You revert back to being a child. It's an escape from life. I really began to fantasize that if only my wife would die we could marry," Steve recalled.

Steve was able to speak frankly about his years of committing incest. Of course, he had been in therapy for many years and the incestuous relationship had stopped long before, so that some of the painful memories had faded.

When his daughter became a teenager, Steve, like so many incestuous fathers, became possessive and jealous, and restricted his daughter's movements. As in many other cases, his daughter began to exhibit signs of trying to break away from her father. Because this relationship had gone on for over five years, she had developed a very close attachment to him. During this time her parents became more and more estranged from each other. She hardly turned to her mother for any type of assistance. Torn between the attachment to her father and wanting out, she finally broke away.

She told a friend. The friend told her own mother, who reported it to the authorities. At first, Steve denied it, then he pleaded guilty to a lesser charge. He never went to prison. Instead he was placed on probation, with the stipulation that he enter therapy.

There is little doubt that Steve is very sorry about what he did. He has continued to take part in a program even though he is no longer required to attend. He is trying to give to the newcomers what he feels had been given to him. He seems to relive a lot of the tragedy. He is trying to give his daughter whatever he can to make up for what he did. He now knows that what he did was wrong, and that he cannot change the past. He cannot give back his daughter's childhood.

He is still in touch with his daughter, who is now an adult and lives with her mother. Steve and his daughter were apparently able to work through some of their relationship, with a great deal of therapy and support from the mother. "My daughter needed to hear that I was really sorry. That I was wrong. And I have told her that hundreds of times by now."

However, according to Steve, his daughter is involved with a type of man who is destructive and irresponsible. She is pregnant and not married. Her boyfriend deserted her just as he was supposed to marry her.

As if in some way he was to blame, Steve is trying to be as supportive of his daughter through this crisis as any father could be.

Steve now lives with his parents and tries to have "normal" relationships with women.

"Are you attracted to young girls?" I asked.

"No, not at all." Steve seems to be drawn to women who were victims of child abuse or incest. Feeling sympathy for them, he tries to make up for what he did to his daughter.

What specifically happened in his life that would explain incest?

"Nothing. Nothing can justify incest. I guess that after the homosexual experience that I had as a teenager, I was afraid that I was "gay." I tried to prove to myself that I was normal. But as my marriage was deteriorating I was too weak to do the manly thing and face my life. I turned to a beautiful child. It was safe and comfortable. I knew that she loved me. We created a real fantasy world."

Dick, Fran's husband, was a bit more like the stereotype of the offender. He was physically large and very domineering. He controlled his family by violence and the threat of violence. He drank heavily, a problem that seems prevalent in over 50 percent of incest cases. His family was his possession; his daughter was a special object that he loved, something that belonged to him.

When the secret was revealed, the daughter was sent to live with the family of her mother's sister in another state. They legally adopted her.

In Dick's case the relationship was one of stepfather and daughter, but he had known the child from the time she was two. In every sense, he was the parental male figure in the household. His daughter, like his wife, submitted to his wishes. Only his opinions mattered.

Like Steve, he had a special relationship with his daughter. He treated her more like a wife, a partner, than he did his own wife. Dick's daughter told no one about the incest.

One day she was in a motorcycle accident with her father. She was taken to a hospital, and while she was there the doctors and a social worker noticed that her father behaved in a way that seemed inappropriate. After she was given a physical examination, it was confirmed that she had had intercourse. She did not deny it.

Unlike Steve's daughter, who has, through therapy, confronted the incestuous relationship, Dick's daughter has yet to discuss the matter. She had not seen her stepfather very much from the time she was placed in the care of her aunt. She is now twenty-one years old and married to an officer in the Navy, a man her mother describes as very strong and domineering—much like her father. Her mother tearfully said that she feared for her daughter. "She so much reminds me of myself, what I used to be like."

The daughter is pregnant. Her parents are not sure how much she has told her husband about her past. Dick seemed very anxious that his daughter confront him with what happened. He welcomed the opportunity to bring it out in the open. He wanted her to forgive him. But she is unwilling or unable to talk about it.

"Many other women can only face incest in their twenties or thirties while in therapy." I added, "Perhaps, your daughter will do the same."

"That's what we are afraid of," said Fran sadly. "As for now, she seems to show no anger or outward pain. She just doesn't want to talk about it."

Fran and Dick have continued in therapy. I am told that Dick has changed. He no longer drinks. He isn't violent. He has changed his attitude about his dominant role, though some of his authority is still apparent. He is still an imposing figure in that house. Dick and Fran have two other teenagers, a daughter who is about twelve and a son who is younger.

"Do you see a difference in the way you act with your daughter from the way you acted with your older daughter?"

"Oh, yes," they both answered. The difference seems to be in the distance he keeps from her. This is manifested in physical distance, as well as in less control over her life. If she has questions relating to sexual matters, her mother handles them. With the older daughter, Dick wanted to be her teacher, her educator, and enjoyed talking to her about sex. That used to be part of the seduction, part of getting his daughter sexually aroused.

With his older daughter, he would buy her nightgowns that were very suggestive. Now, if his younger daughter is not fully covered, he mentions the matter to his wife.

"Do you think that Dick is capable of repeating his offense with your younger daughter?" I asked Fran. This is a problem that is very frequent in incestuous families.

She replied with a firm no. "I can see that he simply responds to her as a father. Also, our marriage is not what it was ten years ago. I am not what I was then; I'll never be that again. I was a doormat; now I am a fully responsible adult and wife."

Joe was a particularly interesting case. He was accused of molesting his fourteen-year-old daughter. He appeared so gentle that it was difficult to imagine him as violent, but he claimed that he used to be. He seemed to be a very warm, caring, and affectionate man. I had a hard time feeling any kind of dislike for him, something I found to be very easy to do, listening to men tell their stories of abuse of children, often with very little remorse. I also had a hard time believing that he really could hurt his daughter. Unlike most cases, the abuse happened a couple of times and did not involve intercourse.

"I guess that your story is very different because the relationship didn't go on for years," I noted.

Joe rejected that notion immediately. "It went on for years in my head. I fantasized about it for years."

Joe wouldn't let anyone shy away from hard reality. Divorced, he is in the rare position of having custody of his three children, including the daughter he molested.

"You have changed that much?"

"I have grown. I think about what I was, what I did, and why I did it. I have made changes."

First, Joe stopped drinking. Then, he came to grips with his violence and the violence that surrounded his childhood.

"Throughout my childhood, no one ever talked about anything. Everything was handled through violence. Dialogue or discussion was not in my vocabulary."

Understanding his own behavior was the real change that Joe made. He considered that his actions had been that of a child. He gave a great deal of validity to those experts who believe that the men who commit incest lack the control that comes with being an adult. As adults, we are expected to be able to govern our actions, to consider the consequences of our actions. For example, we might like to hit someone, because we are angry with him, and it would relieve our frustration to be able to do so. But we don't. We control our impulses. That's part of our socialization, like controlling hunger or other desires. That's part of being a responsible adult. In the same manner, some experts argue that those who resort to incest lack the self-control to refrain from committing the act, that they are in some way like children themselves, and that some have serious sexual disorders.

Joe felt that there was a lot of truth to that idea. He felt that incest is a very self-centered act that lacks any concern for the other individual. It is a purely selfish act. He felt that he was acting out a childhood fantasy. His fascination and curiosity about his daughter were more of an adolescent nature that that of an adult.

"My fascination with her body was that of a twelve-year-old boy, not of a grown man. I was a selfish, inconsiderate child."

All of Joe's children live with him. His daughter has no fears concerning her father committing incest again. She dates boys now, and Joe tries to meddle no more than is a parents' perogative. He felt that it was very important to have a healthy relationship with his daughter, and he welcomed the opportunity to take care of the children after his ex-wife seemed to neglect them.

The change in Joe didn't happen overnight. It took years to get the courts to agree that he was a suitable parent.

"When the judge awarded me custody, I got scared. What if it should happen again? I realized it would not happen because I channeled my love toward women. I grew up. I was my daughter's *father*. I now look at her as my beautiful daughter."

In a way, I felt that of all the offenders I interviewed, Joe had come the furthest in working on his problem, learning how to handle stress, and resolving conflicts in a humane, understanding manner.

But most of the men who commit incest are not like Joe. According to Parents United, a family support group that handles the largest number of incest cases in the country, if most of the men are not ordered to do so by the courts, they would not enter therapy. This view is shared by most therapists. Many men have not admitted guilt, unless they have been forced to do so. Some experts say that it is only when the men recognize that they are better off making the confession that they enter therapy. Even those offenders who have been involved with therapy still like to place some of the blame elsewhere. One of the basic goals of therapy is to reach the point where the men can admit that they have committed an act that hurt their child and they are the ones to blame. The child is innocent and is always the victim, regardless of how seductive they may believe the child had been. It takes years for some of the men to reach that point.

One of the last groups of men I talked with was at the Avenel Adult Diagnostic Treatment Center in New Jersey. This is the only place in America where serious male sexual offenders are treated while serving a prison sentence. (There is no program for female sex offenders.) Here, rapists are put together with incest offenders, child molesters, and general sex offenders. Most of the inmates' time is spent in therapy, amid prison surroundings.

All the men I met with confirmed the offender's need for help. All the men were very different from each other—one man was a habitual offender with many previous drug-related offenses; another was a first offender, a musician who had no previous sexual offense; a third man had committed incest with two daughters. What these men had in common was that they could not stop committing the crime. They were compulsive. On their own, they seemed unable to control their actions. They all said that they were not happy to be in prison, but they were glad that now they were in a position to be treated.

While it is unusual to find men in prison for incest, all three of these men were serving at least ten and as many as twenty years.

Incest changes the whole family. Even years later, the memory of incest lingers on. Family relationships are strained and uncomfortable. What most victims wish for is a parent. What most offenders have given up is the beauty of having loved and nurtured children into adulthood. They abused the love that their children had given them.

[52]

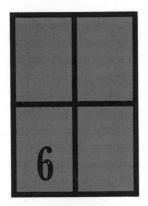

BREAKING
THE SECRET

Sexual relations between adults and children are forbidden by law in every state in the United States. Furthermore, every state has a law specifying that it is mandatory to report cases of child abuse to the appropriate agency. The agency or the reporting procedure may vary from state to state. However, in most states, the law specifies that the privilege of confidentiality between a professional and a client is not sufficient grounds for failure to report a case of child abuse. By definition, incest is child abuse and it is also a crime. What this means in simple terms is that when a child confides in a professional about being a victim of incest, even though she or he may plead for secrecy, the law dictates that the professional must report the case to the proper authorities.

Most incestuous relationships do not meet the legal definition of the crime of "incest." But they fall under the definition of lesser crimes, such as "carnal abuse of a child," or "corrupting the morals of a minor." Incest laws are established primarily to prohibit marriage and inbreeding within families. The definition of incest in many states is restricted to intercourse between blood relatives. Only a handful of states include sexual relations other than intercourse in their incest laws. Less than half of the states include intercourse between stepparent and child in their definitions of incest. However, most states legally recognize a large range of sexual offenses against children other than incest. It is under these laws that some of the incest offenders have been punished.

A 1981 study by the National Center on Child Abuse and Neglect estimates that every year there are almost 45,000 cases of confirmed sexual abuse involving a parent, a guardian, or a caretaker. Most studies, however, suggest that the true incidences are substantially higher, with perhaps 200,000 to 400,000 children being sexually abused annually. In some states, child abuse and child neglect reports have increased over ten times within the past few years. Unfortunately, this tremendous increase in reports is in no way connected to increased staffing or funding of child protection agencies. Therefore, while the law is explicit about what is expected of a social worker, a nurse, a teacher, or any other professional having information of incest, the agencies do not have the necessary funds to handle adequately the number of cases they are expected to process.

Father-daughter incest is believed to be the most frequent form of child sexual abuse nationwide. In 1953, the Kinsey report, one of the most extensive and thorough reports on American sexual behavior, stated that 25 percent of American adult women were molested as children. More than half of the offenders were close friends or relatives. Of this number, 45 percent were fathers.

It would be misleading to suggest that all professionals who are aware of sexual abuse report it to the proper authorities. In fact, I have talked to social workers who admitted to me privately that in some states where supportive programs are unavailable, they first try to handle the case without involving the legal authorities. Some social workers have talked with the mothers privately, hoping that the mothers can handle the situation without legal intervention. Most experts agree that there are serious problems with that approach. Initially, many mothers do not believe that the accusation is true. In that case, the life of the child at home becomes almost unbearable, so that some outside intervention becomes crucial. If the mother is willing to accept that the child is telling the truth, then she is in the most difficult situation of trying to handle the aftermath all by herself. When her child needs an enormous amount of support, she is in the midst of her own crisis.

However, in places that do not have programs that deal specifically with incest, the child protective agencies can be very unpredictable. They may remove the child from the home, which most experts agree is most undesirable, unless the mother is not supportive and will not protect the child. In that case, there is no alternative but to remove the child. If the father remains in the house, the child will not feel secure and safe at home. Therefore, all agree, that once the abuse is reported, the father must leave, even if it's for a short period of time, to enable the child and the mother to confront the situation together and for the safety of the child.

One social worker warned me, "Whatever you suggest in the book regarding how a victim should handle breaking the secret, please be sure to emphasize that while it is very important that the victim tell somebody, it is essential that you explain what happens when the secret is out. That's just the beginning of another ordeal."

Yes, everybody warned me that it is irresponsible not to emphasize firmly that the relief may be temporary. Yet, if the necessary support for the mother and the victim is given, the experience can eventually lead to ending the incestuous relationship and rebuilding the family structure.

When the secret is revealed, the victim needs a great deal of reassurance. First and foremost, the victim needs to be told that the story is believed. Almost all experts agree that children usually do not lie about incest or sexual abuse. Why would they?

Second, a child needs to know and understand that she or he is not to blame, and third, that she or he will be protected from further abuse and that there will be no retaliation for reporting the crime. Also, it is essential that the child understand that incest is a crime and the investigation of incest rests with the officials of law enforcement. However, very often the first question that a child will ask is, "What will happen to my parent?"

They need to know that their parent can be charged with the crime and may be jailed for a short time, but very few serve prison sentences. As the law is written, the punishment for sexual abuse of children may be severe, but in practice, it is almost never carried out.

Almost all experts agree that a prolonged trial, lasting months in some cases, is disastrous for all concerned, particularly the child. If the child has to tell the story to an officer, retell it to a judge, a prosecutor, lawyers, and a full courtroom, with the parent present, clearly it is more than any child can be expected to handle. Many would rather withdraw the testimony. Of course, this is a crime that usually has no witnesses. It is a child's word against an adult's. A prolonged trial makes it almost impossible to get a conviction. Several lawyers stated that they had cases that were thrown out of court because the child got confused and the facts were too vague.

Incest is also difficult to prove in terms of medical evidence. Although there is evidence of the act of sexual intercourse for at least twenty-four to forty-eight hours afterwards, in the case of incest, there may be no sexual activity at the time the child reports it, making it even more difficult for the victim to prove.

When the offender confesses, he begins to take responsibility for his act and in a somewhat indirect way the first part of therapy can begin. Most of the experts believe that how the police play their initial role is crucial. If the offender confesses, often a process of plea bargaining can take place, whereby he can plead to a lesser charge. In that case, the entire family and specifically the child is spared a court trial, an ordeal that is painful for everyone.

However, more and more judges seem to feel some public pressure to give short jail sentences to offenders. And even under the best of circumstances there can be months between the time the abuse is first reported and a final court date or a sentence is set. Most often, the offender is sentenced for a felony, with usually a few months in the county jail, and/or placed on probation for a few years. Sometimes he is ordered to pay a fine and to enter a treatment program. He is also not allowed to see the child for a certain period of time, which may mean a temporary separation from the entire family. Some offenders are sentenced to longer prison terms.

Of course, a child might also decide to tell her mother, who might in turn decide not to report the case to the legal authorities. Certainly, it can be handled as a "family matter." Some people suggest that, in some ways, it may be a better alternative than the ordeal that can come with reporting the crime—the involvement with lawyers, the police, the courts, and the possibility of the parent facing a jail sentence.

I asked one of the offenders if he thought that he should have gone to jail.

He quickly responded, "Absolutely yes. All offenders should go to jail for some period of time."

This man, a grandfather, served a jail sentence at age sixty for the crime he committed against his granddaughter.

"What can jail do for an incest offender?" I wondered.

His answer was that some sort of clear punishment is essential. The few months in jail made him understand that not only did he commit a crime, but that he hurt somebody. He also believed that in jail, separated from his family, he felt some of the pain that he inflicted on his granddaughter.

"You realize that you are a convicted man. You committed a crime. You should be punished. That's part of the therapy. If a man robbed your apartment, took some of your possessions, he would serve time in prison. Incest hurts somebody a lot more than a burglary. It could hurt the kid for life," he said.

At the Harborview Sexual Assault Center in Seattle, Washington, the belief that punishment is essential is stressed. Lucy Berliner, director of Harborview, strongly feels that the child must see that the offender receives some type of punishment. Without that punishment, the child will not see the connection between the harm and the consequence of that act: punishment.

Aside from a possible jail sentence, court-mandated therapy seems crucial for the act to stop. While some try to handle the situation within the family, it is hard to mandate therapy for the offender without some outside intervention.

Once the incest is reported, there are several organizations that can help. The oldest and by far the best-known program in the country is the Child Sexual Abuse Treatment Program in San Jose, California. From an office in the Juvenile Probation Department of the county courthouse, the staff, working with law enforcement authorities, have treated over a thousand families in crisis since 1971. Under a state and federal mandate, the staff trains professionals, including police officers, how to deal with child sexual abuse.

According to the National Center on Child Abuse and Neglect, there are now over 200 programs across the country. About half of them are patterned after the Child Sexual Abuse Treatment Program. Several other programs have developed from rape crisis centers in private institutions or within state agencies that have authority to deal with child abuse.

Parents United is a nationwide program for families coping with the effects of incest and its discovery. A family entering the program is "adopted" by another family who has been in the program for some time. The program is especially supportive of the mother, offering her understanding and reinforcement, so that she in turn can be supportive of her daughter. The stronger the mother feels, the more likely that she will believe that she no longer has to put up with a bad marital relationship.

One mother said that until she entered the program, she never felt a part of any group; she felt isolated. She worked, took care of the household chores, the children, and her husband. She never had time for herself and never felt that she could talk openly with her husband. "Now, I don't feel so alone anymore," she said.

With the help of parent support groups, not only do many of the families stay together (76 percent at Parents United), but some of the women are able to change the structure of their marriage. They feel far less intimidated by their husbands. Now, many of the men seem openly afraid that their wives might leave them. It seems that a shift in power has taken place. Therapy combined with a sense of belonging to a group of women in similar circumstances often give the mothers the self-confidence they never felt before.

But not all mothers choose to enter a support program.

"There is always the possibility of just leaving your husband and taking your children. That is certainly one very real alternative. Not everybody wants to put all their energies into a sick man. You can always leave and the incest will stop," commented a mother who apparently did just that.

"When my daughter told me what had been happening, I confronted my husband immediately. Of course he denied it, but I could tell that he was lying. I sent the kids to my mother who lived in another state, and I left soon after. We never saw him again."

She told her daughter that she never wanted her husband to come back and explained to the younger children that their father was a criminal.

"How did your daughter feel about this situation?" I asked.

She said that she never asked her daughter, but she firmly believed that they were all better off without him.

Although there is no one answer as to how to deal with the problem, almost everyone agrees that as long as the secret is kept, the incest will continue. Revealing the secret is the first and major step toward getting out of a harmful situation. However, there is no general agreement on the best method of exposing the secret. If it is possible to tell the mother, in some ways that may be less difficult than telling a stranger.

"But what if she won't believe you?" asked a young girl.

Of course, in that case it is better to ask for help from a social worker, a teacher, a doctor, or some other professional. The professional in turn can talk to the family. That support may be essential for a child who has difficulty in facing her family. If the offender is the mother, then the child usually has to tell a professional, because there is probably no other adult in the household to tell. In that unusual case, the child is facing the possibility of his mother going to prison and his being placed in foster care.

"Really, removing the boy from that situation is the best thing that can happen. If he is alone with his mother in such a detrimental situation, he is better able to put his life back together away from her," added a social worker.

Except in cases where the other parent is believed to be nonsupportive, most professionals believe that removing the child has terrible consequences. Not only has the child been abused sexually, but she or he is now punished for telling the truth by being taken away from the family and put into a totally new and strange environment.

But when the home environment is negative for the child, and the mother is not giving the support needed, what alternative is there?

A lawyer, who has handled hundreds of child abuse cases, looked at me with some amazement. "What's wrong with a group home? Some of them are excellent. You think that leaving the kid in this environment is better? I think that a group home may be the best thing for that kid. I'm not crazy about these parents. I don't think that they can possibly make their home into a good environment for that kid."

Before a child finally reveals the "secret," it is usually best that she or he finds out what types of programs are available for incestuous families. Many states have programs like Parents United, Parents Anonymous, or Harborview Sexual Assault Center. If there are programs available locally, it is recommended that the child turn to one of these programs for guidance, general support, and therapy. Needless to say, it usually does not happen in such an orderly fashion. When someone finally exposes the secret, the victim is probably not emotionally able to investigate what programs are available.

I heard from victims, offenders, and mothers, "It was the worst day of my life," referring to the day the secret was exposed. The children felt as much anxiety afterwards as the relief they felt in telling someone.

Although it is not the main objective, incest treatment programs also offer the possibility of restoring the family structure. Many victims do not want to see their parents separated. Some feel guilty that they are hurting their parents by exposing them.

Rita said, "Although he was a no-good bastard, he did try to keep us together, which I knew was my mother's wish, and all I could do was picture my father in prison for years to come, without his kids, without anybody. All I could visualize was him sitting in a cell by himself, just thinking, you know. That hurt. I could picture my father going home from work, walking up the stairs to our apartment, opening the door expecting to find us kids running around, and there'd be two detectives waiting to take him to the police station. I didn't like that picture." This is a quote from *Father-Daughter Incest*, by Judith Herman. It is a fear common to incest victims.

All of a sudden, all the threats come alive. "If you tell, I'll kill you," or "Your mother will kill herself." "They'll take you away and lock you up." "They'll put me in prison forever."

With threats like those in the back of their minds it is amazing that kids tell anyone at all. It should be noted that the offenders usually do not kill the children, the mother does not kill herself, the child will not be locked up (although sometimes they are placed in a group home or in a different environment), and the offender does not usually go to prison.

The mother may be very upset, and may even feel that she is about to have a nervous breakdown, but the child is not the one to blame. The child cannot be responsible for the parents' marital problems or one parent's psychological and sexual disorders.

In fact, according to some reports, over 50 percent of the families are restored and the exposed secret is the force behind the parents receiving the needed help.

It is important for incest victims to remember that while they don't want to hurt their parents, they have been hurt by their parents. They cannot protect their parents forever; that kind of protection is not healthy for the family.

"If your father had an illness and you felt that he could be helped, wouldn't you take him to get that help?" said one of the therapists to a victim.

"Of course I would," she replied.

"Your father needs help and you can help him by getting him help. He's a sick man."

The child started to sob; then she nodded her head to signal that she understood the connection.

CONCLUSION

There is little we can say about incest that everyone can agree upon. Perhaps the one major point is that the incest taboo is universal in human cultures. Though there is disagreement as to why the taboo is universal or why it started, it is generally considered by anthropologists to be an essential part of all family structures. Incest is destructive to the family, and if we destroy the notion of family, we place our culture and society in jeopardy.

We can say that incest hurts the victim. The child, harboring anger, guilt, and a frightening secret, experiences immense confusion. Incest defies the belief that the parent is the source of trust, security, and guidance. It confuses the notion of affection and love. It alienates the child from the mother and the father. It accelerates the child's sexual development, and destroys the normal process of sexual maturation and growth.

The most painful part of incest varies from child to child. It depends on the actual experience. Some victims mention fear, while others point to holding on to the secret. Still others mention the feeling of isolation, the inability to feel like a "normal kid." The physical experience, though at times painful, is usually not the worst part of incest. "I couldn't be like everyone else. I felt different," said one of the victims.

Incest also confuses the children because they feel that they were to blame. So often the daughter is accused of being seductive, and she comes to feel that to some degree she "asked for it." Some men have put the blame squarely on the child by making statements like, "She made me do it, she seduced me. I couldn't help myself."

A child should never feel that way. It is always the responsibility of the adult to guide the behavior of the child. If the child acts in an inappropriate way, it is the adult's responsibility to redirect her in the proper manner. She in no way has the power to seduce an adult without the adult being responsible for the act. That's why every state has a law that holds the adult accountable for having sexual relations with a minor.

It is important that a child clearly understand that parents must take responsibility for their actions. They committed a crime. This may also be difficult for the child to accept. Why me? What's wrong with my parents? But as difficult as it is to accept, the child should feel that holding on to this secret is harmful for all.

Whom should the victims tell? There is no one answer to that question. Sometimes it should be the police, sometimes it should be the mother, the father, a teacher, or a doctor. They should tell someone they feel will believe them, someone with whom they feel comfortable.

Children should be taught to protect their bodies. They have to be able to say no to their parents. How can you suggest to a child that she should defy her parent? But in this case, she can and should. Saying no, in many cases, has actually stopped the act.

"Often, if the child refuses, the offender will not pursue the matter," commented a social worker who deals with abused children. "The adult usually turns to a child because he thinks that a child will not reject him. It is a safe place to go. In the case of a male offender, if the child refuses him, it may destroy his ego to try again. So he won't do it again."

However, that's not always the case, but there is some evidence that children just accept whatever is being done to them. In the case of incest, they should have a voice. They have the right to say "No."

It is the feeling of hopelessness that also makes many of the children feel angry with themselves. They feel powerless. That same feeling can continue into adulthood, where they will continue the same submissive behavior. Often, in the case of a girl, she becomes a victim for life by later marrying the same type of man as her father.

In one study of female incest victims, it was found that many of them were also victims of rape later in life. Again, they were put into the position of a victim. They could not say no. They could not fight back. They could not protect themselves, continuing a cycle of low self-esteem and helplessness.

Without fear of contradiction, we can also say that our present criminal justice system is really not the best source for handling the matter of incest. Children should not be subjected to the trauma of participating in a trial, having to tell their story over and over. Once they have given testimony, they should not have to retell the story. Children rarely lie about sexual abuse. Here, we need to protect the victim, not the rights of the offender.

A better way would be to have the child interviewed by someone trained in child psychology or at least sensitive to children's needs and perceptions. The questioning process itself can be so humiliating and confusing for a child that long before the child has to appear in court, she is afraid of the ordeal ahead.

In Denmark and Sweden, authorities have adopted a procedure whereby a social worker and a police woman work together in questioning the child. In Israel, an interviewer, known as a "youth examiner," and trained in both psychology and legal investigation, questions the child. While the youth examiner has broad powers, including determining the course of the case, he or she may at times testify for the child in court, sparing the victim further pain and embarrassment.

The offender should be punished, but prison sentences should not be the only punishment for this crime. It is important that, along with a jail sentence, the offender should receive therapy. As angry as the victims may be, they may not want to put their parents in jail. They just want the parents to stop hurting them. Confinement in jail may be essential for a while, and therapists advocate that it be used to encourage the offender to seek treatment.

We know that incest is far more prevalent than we ever imagined. Sigmund Freud, one of the most distinguished psychologists in history, once believed that incest was a fantasy of children. He argued that they wished for this type of intimacy with their parent. He later admitted that he was wrong. The change from viewing incest as a fantasy to recognizing its very real existence is in itself progress.

Each year more and more cases of incest are reported. I asked numerous experts whether they felt that more incest is being committed or is it just that more of it is being reported. Most of them believe that it is a combination of both factors. Generally, it is believed that because the subject has been receiving more attention, more and more victims are revealing the "secret." Children no longer feel so isolated. They feel that they can come forward, that they may be believed. But other experts suggest that there are more cases of incest today. But since we have little idea of how much of it occurred in the past, there is no way to prove or disprove that theory. However, what some experts fear is that stress is on the increase in our society, and that has an indirect relationship to child abuse. There is more alcohol addiction, more unemployment, more divorce, more poverty, and a record number of people in prison. Some of the frustrations produced by these conditions are taken out on children. Children are easy targets. They won't fight back. They can be easily exploited.

The epidemic divorce rate has also spawned an increase in transient relationships, with frequent partners who may have little commitment to the family and who may lack the social restraints that prevent child abuse. Certainly, as stress increases in society, we will see more incidences of all types of bizarre behavior, incest being one of them.

In fact, the reason that I defined incest in a broad manner is in recognition of the changing American society. Incest is a betrayal of trust. It also negates a healthy relationship between an adult and a maturing child. In a society where over one-third of all marriages will end in divorce, it is essential that we look at the new marital patterns. A child who has lived with a stepfather since age two is expected to respect that authority. When that authority is abused, it is just as confusing for the child as if the offender were her biological father.

A victim pointed out, "I knew this man all my life. Do you think that it made a difference that we were not blood related? It hurt as much, if not more. The only difference I felt was my ability to tell my biological father. I knew that he would go crazy. So, while I wanted to tell him, I was afraid of what he would do. But I could never deny that it was my stepfather who raised me, fed me, took care of me, made me go to school, held my hand when I had my tonsils out; but he also raped me, hurt me, deceived me. The same hurt is there. The guilt is there. The secret is still there."

In this book I have explored and tried to explain the reasons for incest. Why do people do this to their children? What is absent from their character that enables them to commit such an act? Why do men and women feel that they have to turn to their child, instead of another adult? There are many reasons, many different psychological and sexual disorders that lead to incest.

Perhaps we need to concentrate on what a child can do to prevent being placed in the position of a victim. Clearly, a seven- or eight-year-old child will have difficulty refusing to obey an adult, particularly when the act seems to be a gesture of love and affection. But it is important that we instill in our children the belief that their bodies are their own. No one has a right to touch them or feel their private parts. They have control over their bodies, and if someone violates that privacy they should speak out. They should also say no if an adult touches them in a way that they feel is wrong or if they are uncomfortable with the feeling. Children should trust their instincts. They need to learn that if something doesn't feel good, they should tell the adult to stop. If the adult won't, they should tell someone they trust.

It is important to stress that victims of incest shouldn't believe that their lives are ruined. That they feel pain and anger is very understandable, but there are programs that can help them overcome these emotions. Perhaps the greatest help can come from sharing the experience with others who have gone through it.

Incest is adultery, child abuse, betrayal, the breaking of a universal taboo, a crime. It is perhaps one of the most complex acts that we can imagine, but, sadly, it happens all the time. It is to be hoped that one day we will break the unspoken taboo, "the secret," so that we can more effectively enforce the universal taboo of incest.

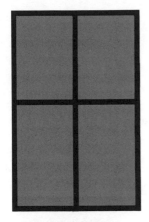

WHERE TO GET HELP

Appendix 1
INCEST PROGRAMS IN
THE UNITED STATES
*Compiled by the National Center
on Child Abuse and Neglect*

ALASKA

Rape Incest Program
Judith Group, Inc.
P.O. Box 2334
Soldotna, AK 99669

Services to parents include alcohol and drug counseling, family counseling, therapy, legal assistance, medical care, employment and housing assistance, transportation, clothing, and food. Services to children include individual therapy, emergency foster care, education, and medical services.

CALIFORNIA

Incest Help, Inc.
719 Jackson Street
Albany, CA 94706

The purpose of the program is to treat and prevent incest. Services to parents include therapy, transportation, and consultation.

Child Abuse Outreach
Foothill Community Mental Health Center
122 West Alosta
Glendora, CA 91790

The purpose of the program is to provide services to families experiencing child abuse and neglect. Services to parents include alcohol and drug counseling; couples and family counseling; social work counseling; and group, individual, and lay therapy. Services to children include individual therapy, art therapy, play therapy, education, and diagnostic services.

Incest Awareness Project
Women's Resource Program
1213 North Highland
Hollywood, CA 90038

Services to parents and families include alcohol and drug counseling, couples counseling, parent aide and lay therapy, legal assistance, employment and housing assistance, crisis counseling, and support groups.

Ananda Marga Family Unity Center
1245 South Norton
Los Angeles, CA 90019

The purpose of this family-oriented program is to prevent and treat all aspects of abuse, neglect, and sexual abuse. A help line ([213] 737-9742) is available for clients.

Sacramento Child Sexual Abuse Treatment Program
5109 Florin-Perkins Road
Sacramento, CA 95826

The purpose of the program is to provide comprehensive therapy to sexually abused children and their families. Services provided include coordination of detection and treatment of incestuous families.

Child Sexual Abuse Program
Family Service Agency
1669 East N.E. Street
San Bernardino, CA 92405

The program provides self-help therapy for victims of incest and their families. A reporting hot line and an information and referral help line ([714] 886-4889) are available.

Child Sexual Abuse Treatment Program
San Diego County Department of Welfare
6950 Levant Street
San Diego, CA 92111

Services to parents include couples and family counseling, group and individual therapy, child management classes, and human sexuality counseling. Services to children include individual therapy, group therapy, and play therapy.

Children's Hospital Child Protection Program
San Diego Children's Hospital and Health Center
8001 Frost Street
San Diego, CA 92123

The purpose of the program is the prevention and treatment of child abuse and neglect. Services to parents include family counseling; individual therapy; parent support groups; and transportation. Services to children include therapy, education, diagnostic services, and medical services.

Santa Clara County Child
    Abuse Program
Santa Clara County Juvenile
    Probation Department
840 Guadalupe Parkway
San Jose, CA 95011

This program provides comprehensive case management of children and families involved in child sexual assault or molestation. The program works closely with self-help groups (Parents United and Daughters United) and provides training and public education.

Child Sexual Abuse Treatment Program
Marin County Department of
    Health and Human Services
San Rafael, Calif. Department of Social Services
P. O. Box 4160
Civic Center Branch
San Rafael, CA 94913

Services to parents and families include couples and family counseling and individual therapy. Services to children include individual therapy and play therapy.

CONNECTICUT

Sexual Trauma Center
139 East Center Street
P.O. Box 551
Manchester, CT 06040

The program provides group and individual therapy for families, children, and adolescents, with an emphasis on male-female therapeutic teams. Play therapy is provided for children and hypnosis and biofeedback are additional therapeutic tools.

FLORIDA

Advocates for Sexually Abused Children
Advocates for Victims
1515 N.W. Seventh Street
Miami, FL 33125

The purpose of the program is to provide treatment to victims of intrafamilial sexual abuse, the nonoffending parent, and the siblings.

Sexual Assault Assistance Project
Palm Beach County
Metropolitan Criminal Justice Planning Unit
307 North Dixie Highway
West Palm Beach, FL 33401

The program has been established to help those victims of sexual battery (adult and child), incest (adult and child), and lewd and lascivious assault (child). A reporting hot line and an information help line ([305] 262-RAPE) are provided.

IDAHO

Incest Program
Idaho State Department of
    Health and Welfare
Pocatello Mental Health Unit
431 Memorial Drive
Pocatello, ID 83201

The program provides mental health treatment services for all members of families affected by incest. Services to parents include family counseling, and group and individual therapy. Direct services to children include individual therapy and play therapy.

ILLINOIS

Child Sexual Abuse Treatment and
    Training Center (CSATC)
345 Manor Court
Bolingbrook, IL 60439

The purpose of the program is to support and treat victims of incest and their families. Services to parents include individual and family counseling, therapy, family planning assistance, babysitting, transportation, and Parents United. Services to children include individual therapy, play therapy, diagnostic services, emergency services, and group therapy.

Child Abuse Unit for Studies, Education
    and Services (CAUSES)
836 West Wellington Avenue
Chicago, IL 60657

The purpose of the program is to prevent severe problems in child rearing, especially abuse and neglect, including sexual abuse and incest. Services to parents and families include couples and family counseling; group and individual therapy; employment, financial, and housing assistance; babysitting; and transportation. Services to children include therapy, diagnostic services, and emergency services.

INDIANA

Child Sexual Abuse Component
Marion County Department of Public Welfare
145 South Meridian Street
Indianapolis, IN 46225

Services to parents include alcohol counseling, couples and family counseling, group and individual therapy, medical and residential care, employment, financial, and housing assistance, and family planning assistance. Services to children include individual therapy, emergency foster care, family foster care, diagnostic services, medical services, and emergency services. A hot line ([317] 236-3911) is available.

IOWA

Domestic Violence Program
Catholic Social Services
315 West Pierce
Council Bluffs, IA 51501

The program provides prevention, information, and crisis intervention. A counseling and crisis intervention help line is operated by the program ([712] 328-0266).

Counseling for Sexual Abuse
Catholic Charities Diocese of Sioux City, Iowa, Inc.
1825 Jackson Street
Sioux City, IA 51104

The purpose of the program is to provide intensive group counseling to female adolescent victims of incest. Services for parents include family counseling, group therapy, and individual therapy. Services for children include individual therapy, play therapy, diagnostic services, and group therapy.

KANSAS

Victims of Intra-Family Sexual Abuse (VISA)
Wyandot Mental Health Center
36th and Eaton
Kansas City, KS 66103

The program provides therapeutic services to all members of families in which child sexual abuse has occurred. The primary objectives are to reduce trauma, resolve underlying reasons for the abuse, and help rebuild a healthy family unit.

MARYLAND

Sexual Abuse Treatment Program
Baltimore City Department of
    Social Services, Md,
312 E. Oliver Street
Baltimore, MD 21202

The purpose of the program is to provide crisis intervention and long-term treatment to sexually abused children and their families. A hot line ([301] 234-2235) is operated for reporting, information dissemination, and referral purposes.

Prince George's Hospital
    Sexual Assault Center
Prince George's General Hospital
    and Medical Center
Department of Psychiatry
Hospital Drive
Cheverly, MD 20785

The program treats incest victims and their families, including crisis intervention counseling, medical treatment, and follow-up services, with a focus on the protection and welfare of the child.

Family Assessment and Treatment Program:
Child Sexual Abuse
Montgomery County Department
    of Social Services
5630 Fishers Lane
Rockville, MD 20852

The program assists in investigations of child sexual abuse cases, including incest. Services include counseling, group and individual therapy, legal assistance, medical care, residential care, homemaker services, and transportation.

MICHIGAN

Community Counseling and
    Personal Growth Ministry
540 Cherry S.E.
Grand Rapids, MI 49503

The purpose of the program is to provide counseling services to families that have experienced abuse or neglect. The primary focus is on incest and sexual abuse. Services to parents include alcohol counseling, couples and family counseling, and individual and group therapy. Services to children include individual therapy and group therapy.

MINNESOTA

Judson Family Center
4101 Harriet Avenue South
Minneapolis, MN 55409

The purpose of the program is to identify, diagnose and treat individuals, couples, and families formerly or currently involved in sexually abusive relationships with family members and to provide training and consultation for professional groups engaged in the identification, diagnosis, or treatment of family sexual abuse.

Southside Family Nurturing Center
2448 18th Avenue South
Minneapolis, MN 55404

The program is focused on the prevention and treatment of child abuse and neglect; it focuses on the whole family in order to improve parent-child interactions. Services include counseling; group and individual therapy; family planning assistance; babysitting; child management classes; and transportation.

Kanabec County Social Services
Kanabec County Department
   of Public Welfare
19 North Vine
Mora, MN 55051

The program is partially concerned with abused and ne-
glected children and their families. Services to families include individual, group, and family counseling; homemaker
services, health counseling, employment assistance, family
planning assistance, medical care, and residential care. An
incest treatment program is available through the Regional
Mental Health Center.

Family Incest Project
Wilder Child Guidance Clinic
919 LaFond
St. Paul, MN 55104

The purpose of the program is to provide services for all
members of families affected by sexual abuse or incest. Services include counseling, group and individual therapy, and
babysitting.

Family Sexual Abuse Treatment
   and Training Program
Meta Resources
821 Raymond Avenue
St. Paul, MN 55114

Services to families include alcohol and drug counseling,
couples and family counseling, social work counseling, 24-
hour counseling, group and individual therapy, lay therapy,
child management classes, and sex therapy. Services to children include individual therapy, play therapy, and diagnostic
services.

Interagency Identification, Intervention,
and Treatment of Incest
Winona Marriage and Family Counseling Service
Winona County Department of Social Services
157 Lafayette Street
Winona, MN 55987

The program provides total family therapy with a nonpunitive orientation. Services to families include couples and family counseling, social work counseling, 24-hour counseling, group and individual therapy, and lay therapy. Services to children include individual therapy and play therapy.

NEBRASKA

Cat and Mouse
Girls Club of Omaha, Nebr.
3706 Lake Street
Omaha, NE 68111

The program's primary purpose is the prevention of child sexual abuse. Services to parents include alcohol and drug counseling, family counseling, social work counseling, group and individual therapy, employment assistance, and transportation. Services to children include individual therapy, art and play therapy, and education.

NEW JERSEY

Incest Counseling Unit
New Jersey State Div. of Youth and Family Services
Mercer County District Office
1901 North Olden Avenue
Trenton, NJ 08618

Services to family members include couples and family counseling, social work counseling, 24-hour emergency response, group and individual therapy, homemaker services, and Parents United. Services to children include individual therapy, day care, group therapy, and family foster care.

NEW YORK

Parent-Child Center
Volunteer Counseling Service
    of Rockland County, Inc.
151 South Main Street
New City, NY 10956

The purpose of the program is to help prevent cruelty to children through counseling. Children receive individual therapy and education. Groups are organized for adolescents who have experienced incest.

VOICES (Victims of Incest Can Emerge Survivors)
Friends Meeting House
15 Rutherford Place
New York, NY 10003

Services provided by the program include assistance for establishing peer support groups, conducting workshops for staff training of personnel in agencies, disseminating public awareness materials, and coordinating with other incest survivor groups in the Northeastern United States and with some international groups.

Alliance—Catholic Charities
1654 West Onondaga Street
Syracuse, NY 13204

The purpose of this program is to provide treatment for families involved with incest.

Victims of Incest
Westchester Jewish Community Services
172 South Broadway
White Plains, NY 10605

Services to parents include alcohol and drug counseling, couples and family counseling, social work counseling, group and individual therapy, employment and financial assistance, family planning assistance, and homemaker services. Services to children include individual and group therapy, play therapy, education, and diagnostic services.

NORTH DAKOTA

Social and Rehabilitation Services Center
North Dakota Department of Human Services
Bismarck, West Central HSC Regional Office
State Capitol, Bismarck, ND 58505

The program's purpose is to prevent and treat child abuse and neglect through provision of appropriate services. The main services for parents are social work counseling, individual therapy, family therapy, couples counseling, and group counseling. Services for children include individual therapy, play therapy, family therapy and group counseling.

Sexual Assault Program
Rape and Abuse Crisis Center
P.O. Box 1655
Fargo, ND 58107

The purpose of a portion of the program is to help sexually abused children and their families. Services to parents include family counseling, 24-hour counseling, and individual therapy. Services to children include individual therapy and play therapy.

OREGON

Christian Family Services
1501 Pearl
Eugene, OR 97401

The purpose of the program is to provide services to victims
of sexual abuse and their families. Services to parents include
couples and family counseling, and individual therapy. Services to children include individual therapy, play therapy, play
therapy groups, education, diagnostic services, and emergency services.

Incest Treatment Program
Malheur County Mental Health and Counseling Center
1188 S.W. 4th Street
Ontario, OR 97914

Services to parents include couples and family counseling,
group and individual therapy, family planning assistance, and
child management classes. Services to children include individual and group therapy, art and play therapy, education,
diagnostic services, and emergency services.

Child Incest Treatment Program
Parents United, Inc.
3905 S.E. Belmont
Suite 1
Portland, OR 97214

The program provides self-help structured treatment groups
for adults and children who have experienced intrafamily child
sexual abuse. Services to families include couples counseling, social work counseling, group therapy, lay therapy, and
child management classes. Services to children include art and
play therapy.

Mid Valley Center Against Domestic
    and Sexual Violence
1244 State
Salem, OR 97301

The program offers crisis intervention and other services to victims of domestic violence, rape, and incest. The program operates an information, referral, and crisis intervention help line ([503] 399-7722).

PENNSYLVANIA

Incest and Sexual Abuse Program
Joseph J. Peters Inst.
112 S. 16th St.
Philadelphia, PA 19102

The purpose of the program is to provide social and psychiatric services to victims of sexual assault and to sex offenders, and to improve the medical, social, and criminal justice system's handling of sexual assault through training, evaluation, research and consultation.

Protective Services
Agency for Children and Youth
P.O. Box 766
Wellsboro, PA 16901

Referrals of neglecting and abusing families are channeled through the agency's existing intake process which includes information and referral and service planning. Emergency services such as investigation of referrals, medical services, emergency caretaker services and shelter care are available on a 24-hour basis. Specialized services include a support group for incest-sexual abuse victims.

TENNESSEE

Project Against Sexual Abuse
   of Appalachian Children
Child and Family Services
   of Knox County, Inc.
114 Dameron Avenue
Knoxville, TN 37917

The program provides rehabilitation services for childhood sexual abusers, their victims, and their families, with a primary focus on incestuous families.

VIRGINIA

Parents United-Fredericksburg Chapter
Fifteenth District Court Service Unit
601 Caroline Street
Fredericksburg, VA 22401

The purpose of the program is to provide an alternative to incarceration for perpetrators of incest and to help affected families cope with the effects of incest and its discovery.

WASHINGTON

Youth Eastside Services
247 100 Avenue, N.E.
Bellevue, WA 98004

Services to parents and families include alcohol and drug counseling; couples and family counseling; and group and individual therapy.

Services to children include individual therapy, foster care, group therapy, play therapy, education, crisis services, day treatment services, incest victims group, drug education and treatment, and diagnostic services.

Incest Treatment Program
Family Services of King County
31003 18th Avenue South
Federal Way, WA 98003

Services to parents include couples and family counseling, and group and individual therapy.

Services to children include individual therapy and play therapy.

Incest Family Services
P.O. Box 44608
Tacoma, WA 98444

The purpose of the program is to treat perpetrators of incest and their spouses.

Services to parents include couples counseling, group and individual therapy, assertiveness and parenting skills training.

WISCONSIN

Child and Family Services
Dane County Department
    of Social Services
1202 Northport Drive
Madison, WI 53704

Services to families include counseling, group and individual therapy, Parents Anonymous, legal assistance, financial assistance, homemaker services, housing assistance, and transportation.

Services to children include individual therapy, day care, emergency and family foster care, crisis nursery, play and speech therapy, education, diagnostic services, medical services, and emergency services.

Rape Crisis Center
Rape Crisis Center, Inc.
312 East Wilson Street
Madison, WI 53703

Services to families include couples and family counseling, babysitting, transportation, and paralegal services. Services to children include counseling, paralegal services, and emergency services. The Center offers two support groups—one for adult and another for female victims of incest from ages nine to twelve. A crisis line is open from 7 p.m. to 7 a.m. every night.

Incest Treatment Service
Family Hospital
2711 West Wells Street
Milwaukee, WI 53208

Services on a 24-hour basis to parents include couples and family counseling, medical care, and family planning assistance. Services to children include day care, medical services, and emergency services. A help line ([414] 937-2180) is available for counseling, information, crisis intervention, and referral.

Appendix II
CHILD SEXUAL ABUSE
TREATMENT PROGRAMS
Compiled by Parents United, Inc.

ALASKA

Anchorage

Parents United
Suite 8
303 E. 15th Terrace
Anchorage, AK 95501
407/267-6440

Fairbanks

Fairbanks Interagency Child
    Sexual Abuse Program
809 College Road
Fairbanks, AK 99701
907/456-2868

ARIZONA

Bisbee

Cochise Community
    Counseling Services
P.O. Drawer GD
Bisbee, AZ 86503
602/432-5484

Coolidge

Department of Economic
    Security
P.O. Box 577
Coolidge, AZ 84228
602/723-5351

Phoenix

Child Protective Services
3727 E. McDowell Rd.
Phoenix, AZ 85008
602/244-8855

Tucson

Child Protective Services
4901 E. 5th
Tucson, AZ 84228
602/723-5351

Yuma

Children's Village
257 South Third Avenue
Yuma, AZ 85364
602/783-2394

ARKANSAS

Child Sexual Abuse
    Program
P.O. Box 1766
Little Rock, AR 72203
501/370-5806

CALIFORNIA

ALAMEDA COUNTY

Emergency Response Unit
La Vista Unit 2
2300 Fairmont Dr.
San Leandro, CA 94578
415/483-9300

BUTTE COUNTY

Emmett G. Anderson, Ph.D.
P.O. Box 4128
Chico, CA 95926
916/891-0674

CONTRA COSTA COUNTY

Child and Family Therapy
    Center
1210 Alhambra
Martinez, CA 94553
415/229-4090

HUMBOLDT COUNTY

Ron Kokish
P.O. Box 3752
Eureka, CA 95501
707/445-6180

IMPERIAL COUNTY

Child Abuse Prevention
  Council
480 Olive Ave., Suite 4
El Centro, CA 92243
619/353-4780

KERN COUNTY

Kern County Mental Health
1960 Flower St.
Bakersfield, CA 93305
805/861-2251

LOS ANGELES COUNTY

Los Angeles

Dept. of Children's Services
Child Sexual Abuse
  Program
54-27 East Whittier Blvd.
Los Angeles, CA 90022
213/727-4281

Lancaster

Child Sexual Abuse
  Program
P.O. Box 922
Montebello, CA 90640-0922
213/727-4281

Long Beach

Child Sexual Abuse
  Program
P.O. Box 922
Montebello, CA 90640-0922
213/727-4281

[88]

Montebello

Child Sexual Abuse
  Program
P.O. Box 922
Montebello, CA 90640-0922
213/727-4281

Paramount

Child Sexual Abuse
  Program
P.O. Box 922
Montebello, CA 90640-0922
213/727-4281

Pomona

Child Sexual Abuse
  Program
P.O. Box 922
Montebello, CA 90640-0922
213/727-4281

Van Nuys

Child Sexual Abuse
  Program
P.O. Box 922
Montebello, CA 90022
213/727-4281

UCLA

Neuro Psychiatric Institute
750 Westwood Plaza
Los Angeles, CA 90024
213/825-0102

MARIN COUNTY

Parents United
50 Nova Albion Way
#107
San Rafael, CA 94903
415/499-8490

MENDOCINO COUNTY

Parents United
747 S. State St.
Ukiah, CA 95482
707/468-4351

Mental Health
860A N. Bush Street
Ukiah, CA 95482

NAPA COUNTY

Mental Health Outpatient
Services
2344 Old Sonoma Rd.
Napa, CA 94558
707/253-4306

Child Protective Services
2261 Elm Street
Napa, CA 94558
707/253-4261

NEVADA COUNTY

Department of Social
Services
10433 Willow Valley Rd.
P.O. Box 1210
Nevada City, CA 95959
916/265-1340

ORANGE COUNTY

Family Services Association
17421 Irvine Blvd.
Tustin, CA 92680
714/838-7377

PLACER COUNTY

Department of Public
Welfare
11519 Avenue B
Auburn, CA 95603
916/783-0401

RIVERSIDE COUNTY

Coachella Valley

Family Counseling
Service of
Coachella Valley
82-380 Miles Avenue
Indio, CA 92201
619/347-2397

Riverside

Associates in Counseling
Suite 339
Riverside, CA 92506
714/682-7844

SAN BERNARDINO COUNTY

San Bernardino

Family Service
1669 N.E. Street
San Bernardino, CA 92405
714/886-6502

Victorville

Child Protective Services
16534 Victor Street
Victorville, CA 92392
619/243-2280

SAN DIEGO COUNTY

El Cajon

Psychological Services,
#250
9455 Ridgehaven Ct.
San Diego, CA 92123
619/569-2055

Escondido

Escondido Youth
  Encounter
165 E. Lincoln Ave.
Escondido, CA 92025

Mira Mesa

Center for Family
  Development
#204
9606 Tierra Grande
San Diego, CA 92126

San Diego

Dependent Children
Department of Public
  Welfare
6950 Levant Street
San Diego, CA 92111
619/560-2236
619/560-2371

San Luis Rey

Center for Family
  Development
800 Grand Avenue
Carlsbad, CA 92008
619/729-9255

David Laratoney
619/757-1200

SAN JOAQUIN COUNTY

Child Protective Services
Drawer F
Stockton, CA 95210
209/944-2069

SAN MATEO COUNTY

Department of Health
  and Welfare
225 W. 37th Avenue
San Mateo, CA 94033
415/573-2041

Family Service Agency
1870 El Camino Real
Burlingame, CA 94010
415/692-0555

SANTA BARBARA COUNTY

Santa Barbara Social
  Services
509 W. Morrison St.
Santa Maria, CA 93454
805/925-0911

Santa Barbara

Child Protective Services
924 Anacapa St.
Santa Barbara, CA 93101
805/963-6101

SANTA CLARA COUNTY

Institute for the
  Community as
  Extended Family
  (ICEF)
P.O. Box 952
San Jose, CA 95108
408/280-5055

SANTA CRUZ COUNTY

Parent's Center
530 Soquel Avenue
Santa Cruz, CA 95062
408/426-7322

SHASTA COUNTY

Welfare Department
P.O. Box 6005
Redding, CA 96099
916/246-5626

SISKIYOU COUNTY

Siskiyou County Mental
  Health
1109 S. Mt. Shasta Blvd.
Mt. Shasta, CA 96069
916/842-3569

SOLANO COUNTY

Mental Health
1408 Pennsylvania
Fairfield, CA 94533
707/429-6521

SONOMA COUNTY

Child Protective Services
P.O. Box 1539
Santa Rosa, CA 95402
707/527-2246

Martha Hyland
Peter Holbrook
707/527-2763

STANISLAUS COUNTY

Incest Treatment Team
Stanislaus Mental Health
1127 13th Street
Modesto, CA 95350
209/571-6100

TULARE COUNTY

Tulare Youth Service
  Bureau
P.O. Box 202
Tulare, CA 92374
209/688-2044

TUOLUMNE COUNTY

Children's Advisory
  Council
c/o County Welfare
105 E. Hospital Road
Sonora, CA 95370
209/533-5860

Ventura County

Simi Valley Mental Health
   Children's Services
3150 Los Angeles Ave.
Simi Valley, CA 93065
805/527-6430 x. 1375

COLORADO

Boulder Council
Department of Social
   Services
Sexual Abuse Team
3400 N. Broadway
Boulder, CO 80302
303/441-1240

DELAWARE

Division of Child Protective
   Services
Children's Service Center
62 Rockford Rd.
Wilmington, DE 19806
302/571-3824

FLORIDA

Alachua County

Parents United
606 SW 3rd Ave.
Gainesville, FL 32601
904/377-7273

Miami

Advocates for Sexually
   Abused Children
1515 NW 7th St., Ste. 112
Miami, FL 33125
305/547-7033

HAWAII

Catholic Social Services
250 S. Vineyard
Honolulu, HI 96613
808/537-6321

Oahu Br. Administration
1060 Bishop St., 5th Fl.
Honolulu, HI 96813
808/548-5344

IDAHO

Boise

Department of Health and
   Welfare Region IV
1105 S. Orchard St.
Boise, ID 83705
208/338-7215

Pocatello

Community Task Force on
   Child Sexual Abuse
P.O. Box 4166
Pocatello, ID 83201
208/236-6006

ILLINOIS

Bolingbrook

Child Sex Abuse Treatment
and Training Center
of Illinois
345 Manor Court
Bolingbrook, IL 60439
312/739-0491

La Salle

Mental Health Center
1000 E. Norris Drive
Ottawa, IL 61350
815/434-4727

IOWA

Ames

Central Iowa Mental Health
Center
713 S. Duff
Ames, IA 50010
515/232-5811

Council Bluffs

Domestic Violence
Program
315 W. Pierce
Council Bluffs, IA 51501
712/328-3087

Iowa Department of Social
Services
12 Scott Street
Council Bluffs, IA 50501
712/328-5689

North Central Iowa

Counseling Association of
North Central Iowa
215 State Street
Garner, IA 50438
515/923-3478

West Branch

Families, Inc.
101 E. Main Street
West Branch, IA 52358
319/643-2532

KANSAS

Johnson County Mental
Health
15580 South 169th
Olathe, KS 66062
913/782-2100

LOUISIANA

New Orleans Police
Department
Child Abuse Unit
715 S. Broad, Rm. 301A
New Orleans, LA 70119
504/586-3184

MAINE

Community Counseling
Center
P.O. Box 4016
Portland, ME 04101
207/774-5727

MARYLAND

Baltimore

Mary Reagan
5735 New Holme Ave.
Baltimore, MD 21206
301/488-1789

Kensington

Linda Blick
1605 Concord St.
Suite 207
Kensington, MD 20895
301/949-3960

MASSACHUSETTS

Department of Social
   Services
143 Main Street
Brockton, MA 02401
617/584-0980

MICHIGAN

Bay City

Lutheran Child and Family
   Service
P.O. Box 8
522 N. Madison
Bay City, MI 48707
517/892-1539

Grand Rapids

YWCA Child Sexual Abuse
   Center
25 Sheldon Blvd., S.E.
Grand Rapids, MI 49503
616/459-4681

MISSOURI

Alpha Counseling
P.O. Box 484, Station F
St. Joseph, MO 64506
816/279-4116

NEBRASKA

Grand Island

Child Protective Services
205 West 1st St.
Grand Island, NE 68802
308/381-5600

Kearney

South Central Community
   Mental Health
3710 Central Avenue
Kearney, NE 68847
308/237-5951

Omaha

Parents Anonymous
711 N. 21st St.
Omaha, NE 68102
402/346-6311

Papillion

Sarpy County Social
 Services
1209 Golden Gate Dr.
Papillion, NE 68046
402/339-4294

NEW JERSEY

Mt. Holly

Division of Youth and
 Family Services
50 Canocas Road
Mt. Holly, NJ 08060
609/267-7550

Trenton

Division of Youth and
 Family Services
1901 N. Olden Avenue
Trenton, NJ 08618
609/984-6300

Ken Singer
609/984-6300

NEVADA

Las Vegas

Nevada State Welfare
 Division
700 Belrose Street
Las Vegas, NV 89107
701/385-0133

Reno

Washoe County Welfare
P.O. Box 11130
Reno, NV 89520
702/785-5611

NORTH DAKOTA

Bismarck

West Central Human
 Service Center
600 S. 2nd Street
Bismarck, ND 58501
701/253-3090

Devils Lake

Lake Region Human
 Service Center
Highway 2 West
Devils Lake, ND 58301
701/662-4943

OKLAHOMA

Family and Children's
 Service
650 S. Peoria St.
Tulsa, OK 75120
918/587-9471

OREGON

Eugene

Children's Services
1102 Lincoln Street
Eugene, OR 97402
503/686-7535

Children's Services
P.O. Box 189
Grants Pass, OR 97526
503/474-3120

Hillsboro

Children's Services
1665 SE Enterprise Ctr.
Hillsboro, OR 97123
503/648-8951

Medford

Children's Services
650 Royal Avenue
Medford, OR 97501
503/775-6120

Ontario

Children's Services
P.O. Box 927
Ontario, OR 97914
503/889-9194

Portland

Parent's United of Portland,
 Inc.
3905 S.E. Belmont, #1
Portland, OR 97214
503/238-9714

Roseburg

District Attorney
Court House
Roseburg, OR 97470
503/672-3845

Parole and Probation
1937 W. Harvard Blvd.
Roseburg, OR 97470
503/440-3373

St. Helens

Children's Service Division
202 Sykes Road
P.O. Box 807
St. Helens, OR 97051
503/397-3292

Tillamook

Corrections Division
2108 4th St.
Tillamook, OR 97141
503/842-8871

PENNSYLVANIA

Parents United
#1718
429 Forbes Avenue
Pittsburgh, PA 15222
412/562-9440

RHODE ISLAND

The Sexual Abuse Project
Bradley Hospital
1011 Memorial Parkway
E. Providence, RI 02915
401/434-3400 x. 106

SOUTH CAROLINA

Mental Health Nurse
  Specialist
People Helpers
206 W. Richardson St.
Summerville, SC 29483
803/873-8483
Hotline: 803/871-9445

TEXAS

Amarillo

Potter-Randall Child
  Welfare
P.O. Box 3700
Amarillo, TX 79106
806/376-7214

Ft. Worth

Family Alliance Center,
  #103
1025 S. Jennings Ave.
Ft. Worth, TX 76104
817/524-3881; 522-6017

Houston

Family Service Center
3635 W. Dallas
Houston, TX 77019

San Antonio

Family Service Association
230 Peredia Street
San Antonio, TX 78210
512/226-3391

UTAH

Logan

Child & Family Support
  Center
149 West 300 North
Logan, UT 84321
801/752-8880

Ogden

Family Support Center
6222 23rd Street
Ogden, UT 84401
801/393-3113

Salt Lake City

Families United
38 W. 3450 S. Main
Salt Lake City, UT 84115
801/446-8353

VIRGINIA

Fairfax

Child Protective Services
4041 University Drive
Fairfax, VA 22044
703/385-8883

Norfolk

Family Services
920 S. Jefferson
Roanoke, VA 24016
703/344-3253

Portsmouth

Tom Gregory
700 North Street
Portsmouth, VA 23704
804/539-0216

Suffolk

Child Protective Services
  Coordinator
Suffolk DSS
P.O. Box 1818
Suffolk, VA 23434
804/539-0216

Virginia Beach

Fae Deaton
1176 Pickette Road
Norfolk, VA 23501
804/623-3890

Dominion Psychiatric
  Associates
1709 First Colonial Ct.
Virginia Beach, VA 23453
804/481-2298

WASHINGTON

Mental Health Center
1321 King Street
Bellingham, WA 98226
206/676-9158

WISCONSIN

Parental Stress Center
1506 Madison Street
Madison, WI 53711
608/251-9464

CANADA

Calgary

Community Treatment for
  Family Sexual Abuse
P.O. Box 1161, Sta. 3
Calgary, Alberta,
Canada
403/272-9149

Oshawa

Grant Fayr
Children's Aid Society
Box 321
Oshawa, Ontario,
Canada, L1V 2P8
416/433-1553

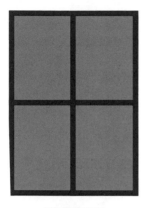

INDEX